Secrets of Superstar Sales Pros

Open More Doors. Close More Sales.

Secrets of Superstar Sales Pros

STRATEGIES FOR SUCCESS FROM
ZIG ZIGLAR, MARY KAY ASH,
JOHN HENRY PATTERSON, AND
THE BEST NAMES IN SALES

Gerhard Gschwandtner
Founder and Publisher of
Selling Power

MCGRAW-HILL

New York   Chicago   San Francisco   Lisbon   London
Madrid   Mexico City   Milan   New Delhi   San Juan
Seoul   Singapore   Sydney   Toronto

The *McGraw-Hill* Companies

1 2 3 4 5 6 7 8 9 0   DOC/DOC   0 9 8 7 6

ISBN-13: 978-0-07-147589-1
ISBN-10:   0-07-147589-3

Contents

INTRODUCTION: STRIVING FOR SUCCESS

YOU CAN'T BECOME successful without first finding an answer to the question "What creates success?"

As you read the advice of the sales professionals and business leaders in this book, do not yield to the temptation to let them answer that question for you. Also, don't try to pick out the raisins. Instead, search for the roots of the grapevine.

Many people believe that they can become successful by imitating the successful habits of superachievers, but this is putting the cart before the horse. Imitation is limitation. People who imitate carry images of only the end product of success in their minds. They stick a picture of yachts or Cadillacs on their mirrors and overlook the crucial difference between the fruits of success and the roots of success. They see the end but not the beginning.

Success begins with the development of your own personal success philosophy. It is your philosophy about your health that guides and shapes your attitudes toward your body. It is your philosophy about money that expands and improves your ability to make money. It is your philosophy about negotiation that creates and builds the tools you use in the negotiation process.

In this book, you will find inspiring accounts of how various leaders struggled to define, adjust, and redefine their own personal success philosophies until they reached their ultimate success.

Look at successful business executives; listen to their advice. You'll find that they spend countless hours and dollars to find the answer to the simple question "What business are we in?" They know that the answer to this key question creates a stable platform from which all corporate decisions can be made to ensure consistency, flexibility, growth, and success.

A business lacking a clearly defined statement of purpose is doomed to fail. Translated to a personal level, if you have failed to consciously define a philosophy of success, you have unconsciously defined a philosophy of failure. This is true simply because, if your life is not guided by philosophy, it will be guided by fantasy. Many people use fantasies or daydreams to protect themselves from reality. They overlook the fact that daydreaming simply amounts to avoiding reality altogether. Well-defined success philosophies will lead to great success in reality, whereas fantasies of success will lead only to greater illusions.

Let go of your daydreaming and you will become successful. In many instances, as you will read in these interviews, reality will far exceed the daydreams you are settling for now.

One more word of caution: Don't limit your success philosophy to a single area. A business can be run on a single statement of purpose; your life cannot. A single success philosophy will get you success in only one area. Success in one area will make you an achiever, not a superachiever.

Learn from the success philosophies of these superachievers, stop dreaming about success, take the first step, and define your own success philosophies. They will become your personal foundation to success.

Keep in mind that it takes no more energy to reach success than to reach failure. This book tells you how to focus your energies to become a superachiever.

Before you read this book, let me warn you again: If you have failed to consciously define a philosophy of success, you have unconsciously defined a philosophy of failure. It's up to you to choose, decide, and then succeed.

PART I

SALES LEADERS IN ACTION

CHAPTER 1

JOHN HENRY PATTERSON

❦━━━━━━❦

He invented the sales manual, the presentation,
the territory, the quota, sales training, and
more. His ideas are still at work today.

T HE GREATEST SALES PRO of all time was born nearly a century and a half ago on a farm in Ohio. His name was John Henry Patterson, and if he were alive today, he'd fire most of the salespeople reading this chapter. Brilliant, innovative, dictatorial, and mercurial, Patterson is best remembered today as the founder of the National Cash Register Company (NCR).

More significantly, but virtually forgotten, this mustachioed, bespectacled whirlwind of a man invented modern selling. The sales training manual, canned presentation, protected territory, and quota system were all products of Patterson's fertile mind. So were sales meetings, direct mail,

Fascinating Fact

After NCR opened a dining room for 400 women in 1895, the sick list dropped from 18 percent to 2 percent in one week.

testimonials, industrial advertising, and publicity.

So numerous were his contributions and vast was his influence that Patterson may rightly be considered the father of professional selling. And perhaps even the father of the modern American corporation, for many of those whom Patterson trained went on to found corporations such as IBM and Burroughs.

 ## ACHIEVEMENT LESSONS

PATTERSON'S SALES INNOVATIONS

- **1884: Exclusive territories.** Patterson purchased the National Cash Register Company and began to hire sales agents across the nation. To create extra incentive, Patterson gave each agent an exclusive territory.
- **1885: Customer testimonials.** Patterson asked his sales force to collect testimonial letters. These letters became the basis of sales brochures that NCR produced for each major industry segment.
- **1887: Sales conventions.** Nine NCR sales agents attended the first sales convention in Dayton, Ohio. The following year Patterson wrote to his agents, "We can assure you that all who will attend, that they will be fitted to sell twice as many registers...." The result: 41 sales agents participated in the three-day event.

- **1888: Direct marketing.** Patterson believed that "sales make news, and the news of sales makes for more sales." He asked NCR agents to collect business cards from their prospects in order to develop a mailing list. In 1888, NCR mailed 135,000 copies of a sales letter that touted the benefits of using an NCR cash register. By 1913, NCR was mailing more than 9 million promotional pieces.

- **1890: Women managers.** Well-educated working women could expect to advance quickly to supervisory jobs within NCR. Amy Acton, who became NCR's counselor-at-law, is believed to be the first woman lawyer hired by a corporation.

- **1892: Sales presentations.** Patterson charged his brother-in-law, Joseph H. Crane, with creating a standardized sales presentation. NCR salespeople were required to memorize the 450-word presentation (and were fired if they refused).

- **1893: Sales training.** Visiting his company's booth at the 1893 World's Fair, Patterson found that NCR salespeople did not know how to sell the cash registers being exhibited. He immediately sequestered the salespeople in a hotel room for a quick training class. This impromptu session was so successful that Patterson instituted regular sales training for all NCR salespeople. Patterson later wrote, "It is said that salesmen are born, not made. I say, salesmen are as you make them."

- **1894: Motivational messages.** Every time Patterson started a meeting, he wrote the word "Think!" on a flip chart. Soon posters with the message "Think" began to appear in NCR offices and on the factory floor. Other motivational messages reminded employees to tell the truth, avoid injuries, and offer suggestions that would improve business.

- **1900: Sales quota system.** Instead of comparing the number of registers sold in each territory, Patterson introduced the revolutionary idea of market penetration. He wrote, "Experience shows that a register can be sold for every 400 people in every town in the U.S." Armed with the latest demographic data on each territory, Patterson developed a fair and equitable sales quota system.

Single-handedly, and often opposed by business associates and the very salespeople who benefited from his genius, Patterson created the greatest selling machine this country had ever seen. It may even be said that no company today approaches the marketplace efficiency that Patterson's NCR achieved in its heyday. Too frequently the practices he pioneered are preached but not followed.

Rest assured that wouldn't be the case if Patterson still walked the earth. Many a head—even illustrious ones—would roll. But sales productivity would soar to peaks not seen in this country since the turn of the century.

> **Fascinating Fact**
>
> *The first NCR factory building was built on the Patterson farm in 1888.*

Few companies have had more inauspicious beginnings than NCR. When Patterson, at the age of 40, bought controlling interest in the failing Dayton, Ohio, firm in 1884, there was really no market demand for cash registers. Fewer than 400 had ever been sold. There were several reasons for this. Few retail businesses, the targeted market, appreciated the value of a device they viewed as a kind of Rube Goldberg machine. Clerks, who felt the cash register represented a mechanical intruder sent to spy on their integrity, were openly hostile to salespeople who came through the door lugging a demonstration cash register. Poor craftsmanship sometimes forced the return of thousands of dollars' worth of machines.

Finally, there was the problem of the salespeople themselves. Solvenly, disorganized, ill prepared, and uncommitted to either the company or product, they almost seemed to stand in the way of sales.

These problems would have sunk most entrepreneurs with a fledgling business, but not Patterson. He was one of those rare human beings whose vision and resoluteness enabled him to divine solutions where others saw only a quagmire of frustration.

An anecdote from Patterson's life illustrates these qualities. Years after NCR was well established, Patterson was told by legal advisors that his plans to incorporate NCR in Ohio would be thwarted by state law unless he reduced the number of people on NCR's board. The wiry Patterson thundered, "Don't change directors. Change the law." They did.

It was with the same single-mindedness that Patterson set out to transform NCR. A sales pro first and foremost, he believed that improving salesmanship was the surest path to success, and that was where he concentrated his efforts. Just as he commanded his attorneys to change a state law, so Patterson set out to change the art of selling.

CREATING A DEMAND

Patterson was one of the first in the country sold—through personal experience—on the value of the cash register. A pair of registers he bought for his retail store cut his debt from $16,000 to $3,000 in six months and helped him show a profit of $5,000. It was that experience that led him to buy the company.

But Patterson was virtually alone as a true believer. So when he bought the company that would become NCR, his first task was to create awareness of and then demand for the product.

Patterson did this in a way that stunned the business community of the day: through the heavy (even relentless) use of advertising, direct mail, and publicity. In so doing, he raised advertising and promotion to unprecedented levels of sophistication, and he created models still in use today.

Often it was a process of trial and error. In his first direct mail effort, Patterson spent thousands of dollars developing a circular for 5,000 prospects. "It was a good piece, but it did not contain a picture of the cash register," said Patterson. Not one response came in to NCR.

Still convinced of the value of direct mail, Patterson continued his experiments, learning as he went and distributing circulars by the millions. Some were in letter form, some carried pictures, others dramatized the use of the cash register. Many were in the form of publications directed to specific groups or retailers. To thwart antagonistic retail clerks, Patterson devised the idea of using plain envelopes, and he often had the pieces mailed from cities other than Dayton.

In an inspired moment, Patterson hit on the idea of incorporating praise from satisfied customers in direct mail. These testimonials proved among the strongest cases ever devised to sway prospects. They were living arguments to buy.

Patterson spent a fortune on paving the way for his sales force through the mail. Stockholders

Fascinating Fact

NCR's millionth machine was manufactured in its Dayton, Ohio, plant in 1911.

and employees tore their hair out at the expense, and the post office had to hire additional postal clerks just to handle the influx from NCR mailings.

Not content to rely on direct mail, Patterson turned his attention to print advertising. At the time, advertising was most notable for its stuffiness, reliance on baroque graphics, and lengthy, tedious copy. Patterson did for advertising what Frank Lloyd Wright did for architecture—simplified it and made it easier on the eye. Not incidentally, he vastly improved its effectiveness.

Patterson's motto for NCR ad copywriters was, "Be direct and simple." Copy was kept brief and to the point. Ads were printed in plain type styles and were broken up with ample blank space. Patterson liked pictures galore in his ads, provided that they were pleasant, upbeat, and "something out of the ordinary" to attract attention.

In conjunction with direct mail and print advertising, Patterson also developed the industrial publicity release. "Business is news," he believed, and so he hired publicists to generate articles by the score on NCR products and activities.

In the end, Patterson's "wild ideas" about promotion were validated. Prospects who had never before heard of the cash register, let alone NCR, were regularly bombarded with a cleverly coordinated mixture of direct mail flyers, print ads, and NCR articles. Those who had previously been unaware of the product suddenly began to develop a need for it.

Unfortunately, the sales force wasn't always in shape to take advantage of Patterson's ingenious efforts. Many knew less about NCR products than did the copywriters!

THE FIRST MODERN SALES FORCE

Early on, Patterson was concerned about the quality of sales, and so—in true Patterson style—he decided to learn firsthand what was happening in the field. In a period of 51 days he visited sales offices in 50 towns and cities. What he found appalled him.

"One half of our salesmen are so ignorant of their product that they will actually prevent a man from buying, even though he wanted a cash register," he said. Returning to Dayton, he proceeded to gather the sales talks of NCR's most successful salespeople, writing up every known selling point for the cash register. The document became one of the first canned sales presentations, the NCR Primer.

Patterson made it a requirement that all salespeople learn the 450-word document by heart. Many of the older salespeople balked. When Patterson discovered their resistance, he implemented tests—those who failed or refused to memorize the Primer were fired. The remainder saw their sales soar. Reason: For the first time ever, they had a consistent presentation that covered all the important features and benefits of their products.

The Primer was soon followed by the Book of Arguments, which later developed into the NCR Manual, a compendium of answers to every kind of question a prospect might ask. The Manual was the first-ever systematic approach to handling customer objections. It also discussed topics such as introductions, first interviews, critical sales situations, and closing arguments. Like the Primer, it was drawn from the minds of the best NCR salespeople and compiled, again, with the goal of establishing consistency.

Many salespeople today would benefit from the wisdom of the NCR Manual. Always it had one objective: to make the prospect understand the proposition, not merely to batter and cajole him or her into placing an order or to win in a series of arguments—still major stumbling blocks today.

THE BIRTH OF SALES TRAINING

Providing the Primer and Manual was one thing; ensuring that salespeople would commit the techniques outlined therein to memory was another. Even with these marvelous tools at their disposal, many balked at learning. It must have seemed to John Patterson that time and again he had to drag mule-headed salespeople to a trough that brimmed with milk and honey.

While attending the 1893 World's Fair in Chicago, Patterson stopped off at the NCR display booths and quizzed the young salesmen. To his astonishment, hardly any of them knew what they were talking about—despite all the sweat he'd devoted to creating the Primer and Manual.

Patterson promptly hauled the reps off to a hotel room for a training session. This class was nothing more nor less than a review of the most basic Q&As about NCR products—material drawn straight from the Primer and Manual. Yet Patterson was so delighted with the results of the impromptu session that he decided to inaugurate training schools for all of his salespeople.

The first sales training school was opened in Dayton the following spring. Though based on the timeworn teacher-pupil format, the classes were as exciting as Patterson himself—a man who once deliberately shattered a water pitcher on a podium to get the audience's attention.

With illustrations and demonstrations (and a good bit of Pattersonian drama tossed in), NCR sales training instructors coached salespeople on the very modern concept of thinking in terms of the prospect's needs rather than in terms of the product. These training sessions were really classes in the art of communication, of understanding prospects and making sure they understood the sales message.

This was a hot topic with Patterson. He was often quoted as saying that fully one half of all lost sales could be attributed to the salesperson's failure to communicate. The erring sales rep might fail to clarify a point, talk indistinctly, make confusing claims or in some way fail to relay his or her own mental picture to the prospect.

Patterson rectified the problem of poor communication by teaching salespeople to listen to prospects. They were taught how to modify set sales presentations depending on the type of customer and the type of sales resistance showed. Patterson even hired elocutionists to teach sales agents to speak like masters of the stage.

A firm believer in "teaching through the eye"—using charts, graphs, drawings, or any other visual aid to get a point across to his sales force—Patterson told salespeople to use the same technique with prospects. Sales agents were schooled in how to "illustrate" a presentation on a scratch pad while they talked about cash registers. Later, outline charts were printed on the pads, which the salesagent would complete as he or she developed his or her presentation.

Thus was born the use of graphics in the sales presentation, an idea used by many but still scorned by some salespeople nearly 100 years after Patterson developed it.

The salespeople turned out by the NCR training school were a well-honed lot. Estimates made at the time show that this training was directly responsible for doubling business in the first year.

THE REWARD SYSTEM

While Patterson demanded much of his salesagents, he gave much in return. Many of his creations, such as the sales convention, the protected territory, and the quota system, were vehicles for rewarding salespeople as well as for increasing productivity.

Patterson was among the first to recognize the value of brainstorming sessions among salespeople. As a result, he decided to conduct regular sales conventions where agents could exchange ideas on selling. In an "every man for himself" era, this was a revolutionary concept. In time, the conventions also provided the opportunity to recognize and reward top achievers.

Patterson developed the protected sales territory in order to attract and keep the best salespeople. In the days B.P. (Before Patterson), salespeople commonly "milked" an area and then moved on—often into a city or region occupied by other cash register salespeople. Needless to say, this chaotic habit of raiding one's colleagues caused a lot of bickering and turnover, and it reduced productivity.

Patterson's solution of setting up protected sales territories is something every salesperson takes for granted today.

In return for this guarantee, NCR agents had to live up to another of Patterson's creations, the sales quota, which was the first effort to obtain measurable results in selling. And they had to try another then unheard-of practice—returning, after a period of time, to customers who had already bought from NCR to try to sell to them again.

Returning to an old customer, a technique Patterson called "using the user," upset many salespeople, who were convinced it was impossible to sell twice to the same prospect. As usual, Patterson was right and the objectors were wrong. Not only did past customers prove a fertile field for new sales, they were also a source of testimonials for advertising and promotions.

PATTERSON'S SIGNIFICANCE TODAY

It's all fine and well to pay tribute to a man like Patterson. Certainly sales professionals and sales managers owe him a debt of gratitude. But after this laudatory display, they would do well to go back and review Patterson's contributions. Not only were his selling techniques the most sophisticated of his day but they are still—in combination—more advanced than anything practiced today. Nobody is this sophisticated now.

Billions are spent on advertising, direct mail, and publicity, but rarely are these tools used as effectively as the cohesive triad Patterson forged. Salespeople still balk at learning product knowledge cold, and they fail to communicate with customers. Though territories are parceled out and quotas maintained, day-to-day sales performance is not monitored as closely as it was at Patterson's NCR.

As the founding father of sales, John **BENCHMARKING**
Henry Patterson used a recipe for success
that remains equally effective today. With product knowledge and
promotion, objection-handling ability, and Patterson's other success ingredients, you can achieve your own modern-day success.
Find out if you have the right stuff—and how to get it—by taking this quiz and the advice you find next to your score.

5 = always, 4 = often, 3 = sometimes,
2 = rarely, 1 = never

1. I use newsletters, direct mail pieces, broadcast faxes, and/or
   other methods to promote my product.

   5   4   3   2   1

2. I read and learn my company and product literature and
   improve my sales techniques with books, tapes, and training
   courses.

   5   4   3   2   1

3. When I learn information I can use to sell, or a new sales technique, I devise practical ways to use it on my next call.

   5   4   3   2   1

4. I am aware of the most common objections to my product
   and the most effective responses.

   5   4   3   2   1

5. I hold regular brainstorming sessions alone or with a group.

   5   4   3   2   1

6. I know how to listen and communicate effectively with
   prospects and use visuals to reinforce my main points.

   5   4   3   2   1

Your total: _____

Your final score: Add your score for each question to get your final score. If you scored:

From 25 to 30 points: You would've been a star player on Patterson's sales team. For continued improvement, use the ideas from your brainstorming sessions to pioneer your own new sales strategies.

From 18 to 24 points: Never underestimate the value of training—even veterans need it. Have your manager select several sales books, and study them to refresh your memory of basic sales techniques and introduce you to new ones.

Below 18 points: Your sales are slipping through the huge gaps in your training. Seek basic training from a professional, and once you learn how to sell your product, let prospects know about it with creatively designed flyers, brochures, and other promotional pieces. Continue to read and learn, and try to perfect a new skill every week or month.

It's a pity, considering the rich heritage John Henry Patterson left to the sales profession. Perhaps more than any other American in history, he is responsible for raising the consciousness, self-image, and public image of salespeople. He taught that good salespeople are made, not born. Patterson transformed an often-ridiculed job into an honored profession, and he gave salespeople the skills to survive in this toughest of all callings.

ACTION PLAN

- Promote your product. To sell his profit-generating cash registers, John Henry Patterson knew he had to spread the word about them. Good promotion tells prospects about your product and why they should buy. How can you get your message out to a larger audience of new prospects and keep current ones informed?
- Invest in education. Patterson pioneered sales training because he knew that salespeople must be informed to be effective. For great salespeople, school is always in session. What people can you talk to, books can you read, or courses can you take to learn more about your products, customers, competitors, and new sales techniques?
- Put lessons into practice. To help salespeople use information in the NCR Primer and NCR Manual, Patterson established training schools that doubled NCR's business. Knowledge must be implemented to make a difference. How can you translate the information you absorb into practical techniques for use on your next call?

CHAPTER 2

DALE CARNEGIE

Nearly half a century after his death, Dale Carnegie's Timeless Teachings can still help you win sales and influence buyers.

THE BROOKLYN BUSINESSMAN, newly enrolled in a Dale Carnegie course, approached the podium to deliver his maiden speech. To this day, people recall how his hands trembled and his face twitched. Reaching the lectern, the Brooklyner turned to face his listeners. He felt like a man under a 1,000-watt light bulb. He unhinged his jaw, but nothing came out. He fainted and crumpled to the floor. In an instant, Dale Carnegie leapt to the platform and swept his hand toward the prostrate body.

> **Fascinating Fact**
>
> *Initially, the YMCA refused to pay Dale Carnegie even $5 a night as a salary.*

"One month from today, this man will make a speech from this platform!" he thundered.

Sure enough, one month later the famous Brooklyn fainter made that speech.

Dale Carnegie—who was this man who inspired hundreds of thousands, and whose message has blossomed and spread in the decades since his death in 1955 to help mold millions of men and women including now-legendary figures like Lee Iacocca, Zig Ziglar, and Ed Foreman?

Like all those who earn "bigger-than-life" status, Carnegie was many people in one: sales pro, brilliant intellect, grassroots philosopher, renowned speaker and innovator, and author of the worldwide best seller *How to Win Friends and Influence People*. A diligent scholar familiar with Shakespeare, Socrates, and Plato. A pragmatist who applied learning to advance his teachings. Friend of presidents, explorers, film stars, writers, and the common person. Equally comfortable in the company of business leaders or heads of state.

More than anything else, Carnegie was a man who believed—and proved countless times over—that the art of communication, learned through the mastery of public speaking and the study of human nature, is the key to prosperity and happiness.

Fascinating Fact

For a while, Carnegie lived in a roach-infested furnished room on West 56th Street in New York City.

THE MAN

J. Oliver Crom, former president of Dale Carnegie & Associates, Inc., in New York, remembers him as a person with innumerable interests, a deep love of life, and a wonderful sense of humor.

"He loved to work in the yard. He was a gardener and loved roses. He was a fantastic photographer, and he loved the theater. He loved museums. He loved everything in life—fishing and hunting and climbing mountains," says Crom.

"He asked questions and listened." In other words, Carnegie practiced what he preached in his famous book and lectures; he showed appreciation for people, made them feel important, and respected the views of others.

Crom has a favorite story that illustrates this quality of Carnegie's:

> He was at a very fancy affair and was seated next to a scientist. Mr. Carnegie knew nothing about this particular science, but throughout the dinner he asked the scientist questions that encouraged him to talk about what he was involved in. At the end of the dinner, the scientist went up to the host and told him that Mr. Carnegie was a most fascinating conversationalist—and all that he'd done was ask questions and listen!

The idea of showing appreciation for others through intent listening was first outlined in Carnegie's lecture (and later book) *How to Win Friends and Influence People*. The book, which has since been printed in nearly 40 languages, made Carnegie an "overnight" success. Of course, like most "overnight" successes, Carnegie's triumph took many years to achieve—24, in fact. During that time, Carnegie developed the ideas that would later form the hub of his teachings. Through an incredible variety of jobs, experiences, and travels, he molded himself into the man who would one day have the ears of millions.

THE MYTH

Like Abe Lincoln, whom he admired (and later wrote a book about), Carnegie had a background from which myths are made—both came from humble origins. Born in 1888, son of an unsuccessful Missouri hog farmer, young Dale rode to school on horseback wearing a pair of pants that pinched and a coat that swallowed him. But even as a youth, he shot off sparks illuminating the brilliant career that lay ahead. In college he so excelled at debating that he was given the job of coaching other members of the debate team.

Beginning in 1908, Carnegie took jobs selling everything from bacon to courses in engineering. He gave up selling temporarily to tour the country as an actor and stage manager. Disappointed with his income, Carnegie augmented his earnings by selling neckties, then chucked both to sell Packard automobiles, a product he amiably admitted he "knew nothing about."

Carnegie's turnaround year was 1912. It was then that he hit on the idea of teaching a course on public speaking at New York City's YMCA. The course was a smash hit, as were the inspirational articles he began to publish. By 1916, he was earning $400 per week, big money for those days, and could call on the likes of Franklin D. Roosevelt, then Navy Secretary, to headline a speaking engagement.

Already, Carnegie was beginning to understand why audiences were drawn to him. "Those adults didn't come to my classes because they wanted college credit or social prestige," Carnegie later recalled. "They wanted to solve their problems. They wanted to be able to stand up on their feet and say a few words at a business meeting without fainting from fright."

ACHIEVEMENT LESSONS

DALE CARNEGIE

- **Dale Carnegie on self-consciousness.**   There is only one person who can cure someone of self-consciousness and that is himself. I know of no other handicap the cure for which can be written in so few words—"Forget yourself." When you are feeling shy, timid, self-conscious, put your mind on something else immediately. If you are speaking, forget everything but the subject. Never mind what others are thinking of you or your delivery; just forget yourself and go ahead.

- **On pep talks.**   Is giving yourself a pep talk every day silly, superficial, childish? No. On the contrary, it is the very essence of sound psychology. "Our life is what our thoughts make it." Those words are just as true today as they were 18 centuries ago when Marcus Aurelius first wrote them in his book *The Meditations.*

- **On opening minds.**   Remember that the man you are talking to is a hundred times more interested in himself and his wants and his problems than he is in you and your problems. His toothache means more to him than a famine in China that kills a million people. A boil on his neck interests him more than 40 earthquakes in Africa. Think of that the next time you start a conversation.

- **On enthusiasm.**   How can you make yourself become enthusiastic? By telling yourself what you like about what you are doing and passing on quickly from the part you don't like to the part you do like. Then act enthusiastic; tell someone about it; let them know why it interests you.

- **On acting.**   If you act "as if" you are interested in your job, that bit of acting will tend to make your interest real. It will also tend to decrease your fatigue, your tensions, and your worries.

- **On perspective.**   About 90 percent of the things in our lives are right and about 10 percent are wrong. If we want to be happy, all we have to do is concentrate on the 90 percent that are right and ignore the 10 percent that are wrong. If we want to be worried and bitter and have stomach ulcers, all we have to do is to concentrate on the 10 percent that are wrong and ignore the 90 percent that are glorious.

- **On enemies.**   When we hate our enemies, we are giving them power over us; power over our sleep, our appetites, our blood pressure, our health, and our happiness. Our enemies would dance with joy if only they knew how they were worrying us, lacerating us, and getting even with us! Our hate is not hurting them at all, but our hate is turning our own days and nights into a hellish turmoil.

- **On selling ideas.**   Don't you have much more faith in ideas that you discover for yourself than in ideas that are handed to you on a silver platter? If so, isn't it bad judgment to try to ram your opinions down the throats of other people? Wouldn't it be wiser to make suggestions – and let the other man think out the conclusion for himself?

- **On worry.**   If you have a worry problem, do these three things:
  1. Ask yourself, "What is the worst that can possibly happen?"
  2. Prepare to accept it if you have to.
  3. Then calmly proceed to improve on the worst.

- **On making friends.**   If you want to win friends, make it a point to remember them. If you remember my name, you pay me a subtle compliment; you indicate that I have made an impression on you. Remember my name and you add to my feeling of importance.

At the same time, Carnegie discovered the technique for getting people to overcome their fear of public speaking. He simply asked them to talk about themselves. "Without knowing what I was doing, I stumbled on the best method of conquering fear," he said.

World War I sidetracked him with a brief Army stint. Afterward, he was off on yet another venture, traveling the globe as Lowell Thomas's business manager. Passing his 30th year, he left Thomas and set out to become a literary legend. However, his novel *Blizzard* was received frostily by publishers.

Like many superachievers, Dale Carnegie was a man leaping from success to success, over the occasional sinkhole of disappointment. He seemed obsessed with launching boldly into new ventures, totally undaunted by the prospect of failure, as if for no other reason than to enrich his life with novel experiences. One might surmise that Carnegie sensed the coming calling of his destiny and that he considered all challenges simply as prerequisite courses.

The stories from this era testify to his exuberant attitude in dealing with roadblocks. There was the time, for instance, that he climbed a telephone pole to sell an engineering course to a lineman. Later selling pork for Armour, Carnegie confronted a merchant who couldn't pay his bill. They struck a bargain. Carnegie took a stack of shoes off the counter, walked down the street to the railway station, and sold them to the railroad laborers. The receipts were forwarded to Armour that afternoon.

Each experience—as a salesperson, actor, business manager, author—contributed to the man who blossomed during the 1920s.

THE MESSAGE

In 1922 he again began to teach, patiently building up his classes in New York. Not discouraged by the failure of his novel, Carnegie resumed writing, turning out innumerable articles and publishing his first successful book, *Lincoln the Unknown*. Soon he was broadcasting his own radio program to millions of listeners.

After several years of teaching, and the 1926 publication of a four-volume work on oratory, Carnegie condensed what he'd learned about his students. It dawned on him that the goal of communication since the eras of Pericles and Cicero had been to influence others. And the most effective communicators had always been those who were not merely good orators but who also understood human nature.

For Carnegie, it was a revelation. The years of experience crystallized into the seed of what was to become the famous Dale Carnegie Course.

Setting out to learn all he could about the art of human relations, Carnegie was amazed to discover that there wasn't a single modern book on the subject. Ever the man to take the initiative, he hired a researcher who spent eight hours a day for 18 solid months plowing through countless thousands of magazine articles—reading everything that had the remotest bearing on the subject of how to win friends and influence people.

Drawing on this raw material and his own rich experience, Carnegie wrote a brief talk, which later evolved into a full-blown lecture entitled "How to Win Friends and Influence People." A Simon & Schuster editor who happened to take the course liked Carnegie's ideas so much he offered him a book contract. The year was 1936, smack in the middle of the Great Depression. Lines of people jamming bookstores for Carnegie's masterpiece may have at times surpassed those at soup kitchens. A half-million copies sold in the first year.

What made the book such a sensation? Carnegie employed a sure-fire formula: Tell the people something that is practical, personal, and optimistic. Keep it simple, and make the goals accessible by using real-life stories as proof that the teachings work. It was a winning formula, and it worked.

Carnegie taught one fundamental lesson: how to deal successfully with others. He trumpeted the principles of how to be a good salesperson of products, services, and ideas.

He made his points unforgettable by telling a story and summing it up with a moral. Whether he was quoting Shakespeare or spinning a yarn about a salesperson, he employed simple language to reinforce universal principles.

This was his genius—drawing attention to the overlooked nugget of truth. What could be more commonplace than his advice "Don't criticize, condemn or complain" or "Become genuinely interested in other people"? Where Carnegie was profound was in his ability to convince people that these gems of wisdom were too often taken for granted.

TIME-TESTED PRINCIPLES

Because Carnegie was a man of action, it's little wonder that his books are "action books" and his lectures "calls to action." *How to Win Friends and Influence People* proceeds from anecdote to anecdote. In case you missed it, Carnegie offers a one-sentence synopsis at the end of each chapter that tells you what to do.

Fascinating Fact

Dale Carnegie once purchased 180-million-year-old dinosaur tracks from the Peabody Museum of Yale University.

"If you want to persuade someone to your point of view, make him feel like somebody," said Carnegie. Put yourself in his shoes. Don't talk—listen to his problems and concerns. Show that you are genuinely interested. Don't argue—respect the opinions of others. Lavish praise for the merest achievement or improvement. Make people happy about helping you. In other words, use the personal touch—that's the way to sell yourself.

Carnegie taught that anyone could learn and follow these ideas, and he went further to say that all successful people do exactly that. In fact, knowledge of human nature is always more important than mere professional or technical skill. The person who masters this wisdom becomes the trusted steward of power.

Carnegie's principal hero in this regard was Charles Schwab, the man chosen by industrialist Andrew Carnegie to run U.S. Steel. Acknowledged as the first executive to earn a million dollars a year, Schwab frequently admitted that there were many people better versed in the steel business. But he gave ground to no one in the field of human relations, where he was an undisputed master.

In his teachings, Dale Carnegie often used a favorite quote of Schwab's: "I consider my ability to arouse enthusiasm among my people the greatest asset I possess, and the way to develop the best that is in a person is by appreciation and encouragement."

DALE CARNEGIE TODAY

Carnegie's teachings are as fresh and inspiring now as on the day he assembled them in the mid-1930s. If he was bigger than life while alive, it may be said that in death he has become an institution. There are two reasons for the continued success of Dale Carnegie. One is the universal appeal of the teachings, which have been expanded to include courses in management training and sales training. The other is the concept of stewardship, which Carnegie's successors put to work within the organization soon after his death.

It's an inspiring story, one J. Oliver Crom relishes telling: "Shortly after Mr. Carnegie died, a group of businesspeople came to Mrs. Carnegie and said, 'We're here to purchase the company—this is what we're offering and you'd better take it.' She turned them down.

"The following June at our convention, Dorothy Carnegie rose before the assembly and said, 'This is a sad time for all of us, following my husband's death. I don't know what you all are planning to do, but I know what I'm planning to do.'

"Talk about inspiration. Everyone wanted to know what they could do to help. And that's when this organization began to take on truly national proportions," says Crom.

Under Dorothy Carnegie's direction, the company introduced stronger, more centralized management and financial planning. It formalized instructor-training programs to ensure the highest-quality hired marketing specialists, and it launched its first national advertising campaign.

All of this was accomplished in the space of one year— 1957. Today, Dale Carnegie & Associates can look with pride on having trained 3,000 instructors offering courses in 1,000 cities. Graduates now number more than 3 million people, compared to 350,000 at the time of Dale Carnegie's death.

Crom attributes this success to Dorothy Carnegie, who ran the company for 20 years. As Crom considers the growth of the organization, he has mused on the "problems" that sometimes attend success. "Our image is so good in the area of public speaking that many people don't realize we also have the other programs to satisfy very special needs within an organization."

Dale Carnegie is alive and well.

Good selling is more about caring than **BENCHMARKING**
closing. Prospects "buy" you as well as
your product—making them feel important makes you hard to
resist. With Dale Carnegie's persistence, interest in others, and
desire to serve, your success odds improve. To get your people
skills up to par, take this benchmark quiz to reveal your strengths
and weaknesses.

5 = always, 4 = often, 3 = sometimes,
2 = rarely,   1 = never

1. I pursue challenging prospects in spite of the possibility of
   failure.

   5   4   3   2   1

2. I make a point of asking buyers about their families and hob-
   bies, and I remember the information they share.

   5   4   3   2   1

3. Instead of trying to impress prospects with my words, I keep
   my language clear and simple.

   5   4   3   2   1

4. I can make a presentation without letting fear sabotage my
   performance.

   5   4   3   2   1

5. On every call, I make my buyer feel important and appreciated.

   5   4   3   2   1

6. I treat all customers with the courtesy and respect they
   deserve.

   5   4   3   2   1

Your total: _____

Your final score: Add your score for each question to get your final score. If you scored:

From 25 to 30 points: You make everyone feel like a million! Keep your selling skills as polished as your relationship skills, and your success is ensured.

From 18 to 24 points: Fear and/or greed may be holding you back. Learn to view challenges as opportunities, and customers as individuals with real emotions who want to feel valued and valuable. On every call, pay your buyer a sincere compliment, or ask about a nonbusiness issue that's of particular interest to them.

Below 18 points: Why so cold? If your customers feel no personal connection to you, another vendor might easily lure them away. Put *How to Win Friends and Influence People* at the top of your reading list, and translate its lessons into specific action steps to use with your prospects and customers.

ACTION PLAN

- Rise to the challenge. Growth comes from testing yourself and taking risks. Dale Carnegie jumped from one new challenge to the next, willing to risk failure for a chance at success. How can you look for new challenges and learn to face them more eagerly?

- Take an interest in others. Carnegie earned praise as a "fascinating conversationalist"—just by listening attentively. Effective customer service starts with salespeople who want to know more about their customers professionally and personally. What can you do to learn more about your buyers and show them you care?

- Keep it simple. Simple, straightforward language makes your message easy to understand. Carnegie used "simple language to reinforce universal principles"—and spoke with greater impact as a result. How can you use terms to show knowledge of your industry, yet keep your message simple?

CHAPTER 3

LILLIAN VERNON

To succeed from scratch, take these lessons from Lillian on how to make decisions, make buyers feel special, and let the entrepreneural spirit move you.

WHAT DO HILLARY CLINTON, Tipper Gore, Frank Sinatra, Betty White, Steven Spielberg, Loretta Lynn, and Arnold Schwarzenegger have in common? In addition to achieving tremendous success in their individual fields, these superstars all number among the millions of customers who have helped build the Lillian Vernon catalog retailer into one of America's most popular and successful direct marketing companies.

But as the woman who single-handedly turned a home-based pet project into a multi-million-dollar company knows, Lillian Vernon did not create phenomenal success by catering to the world's rich and famous. With her genuine entrepreneurial spirit, unique sales savvy, and almost super-human dedication to satisfying every single customer, Lillian Vernon has made her millions by turning the American home into her personal showroom.

 ACHIEVEMENT LESSONS

You can't break Lillian Vernon's entrepreneurial spirit. Her self-motivation, work ethic, and dedication to customers helped turn $2,000 into a multi-million-dollar mailorder empire. As a salesperson, you are also in business for yourself, so follow in her footsteps to foster the entrepreneurial spirit you need to succeed.

- **Be a self-starter.** When you can motivate yourself to action, you hold the key to your own achievement. Vernon had the desire and discipline to build her business without counting on others to get her started and keep her going. Hold yourself responsible for your success, and learn to motivate and discipline yourself to keep moving toward it.

- **Work your way up.** To keep her business afloat, Vernon worked day and night mailing merchandise, writing catalog copy, and conducting financial analysis. For success-bound salespeople, long days are the rule rather than the exception. Be willing to work for what you want, and remind yourself often of the great rewards in store for you.

- **Take your chances.** "I take chances," Vernon says, "by acting on my 'golden gut.'" Entrepreneurs know that growth always involves risk, but they are willing to lose so they can eventually win. Learn to weigh risks carefully and to go out on a limb when the potential gains are worth it.

From the very beginning, Lillian Vernon has stressed personalizing her products to make each customer feel special. In 1951 as a newlywed at home expecting her first child, Vernon used $2,000 of wedding gift money to purchase a supply of belts and purses and to place a $495 advertisement in *Seventeen* magazine offering to personalize orders with her customers' initials free of charge. The response—$32,000 worth of orders from the one ad—would to this day make any direct marketer's mouth water. In her next attempt Vernon added personalized bookmarks, and sales more than doubled.

By 1954 Vernon had begun mailing out a 16-page black-and-white catalog offering combs, blazer buttons, collar pins, and cuff links—all personalized of course. In 1956 she stopped operating the business from her kitchen table and moved into a storefront warehouse with a building next door dedicated to monogramming. Not surprisingly, business continued to boom, and by 1970, the 19-year-old venture known as the "Lillian Vernon Corporation" posted its first million-dollar sales year.

After that amazing year, Vernon realized that to continue growing the business, she would have to delegate some responsibility and adapt the company to address future concerns. "In the early days," she says, "there was nobody else but me to do the work. During the day I mailed out the merchandise, and at night I worked at home doing financial analysis. I did all the buying and wrote the catalog copy; I tried to do it all, and it worked pretty well for the first half of my career.

"But after 1970 I was facing a harsh reality. Growing from a million- to a multi-million-dollar company involved

areas such as finance, list management, and computers. So
I did what needed to be done and did it quickly—I acted.
I filled my ranks with managers from all different walks of
life who generally were very savvy to the ways of big business, and they almost killed us."

Vernon found that despite
their experience, these executives
couldn't act decisively. Instead of
making them into fast-acting
visionaries like their new boss,
corporate America had taught
them to be cautious to a fault.

Fascinating Fact

*Lillian Vernon
mails more than
101 million
catalogs each year.*

"Some of the executives I hired just couldn't make a
decision," Vernon says. "They took analysis to the point of
paralysis. Every major decision had to first be studied by a
committee."

From this experience Vernon learned that her success
stemmed from time-sensitive decision making and rapid
responses to her customers, not from creating committees
to mull over every possible course of action. To grow, she
realized that the Lillian Vernon Corporation would have to
blend the entrepreneurial spirit that built the company into
the professional management techniques that must exist in
a multi-million-dollar company.

"My mistake," she explains, "was not hiring professional
managers; it was letting them work in a nonentrepreneur-
ial fashion. If I've learned anything over the years, it is the
importance of drawing from the best qualities of both
the entrepreneur and the professional manager. These are
the left and right sides of the business brain, and they must
harmonize in a healthy corporation."

Thanks to the integrity, personalized products, and great service she offers customers,

BENCHMARKING

Lillian Vernon takes orders from everyone. To take more orders of
your own, model your success strategy after hers. Put your entrepreneurial spirit and actions to the test, and find out how to adjust
your skills and attitude so that success has your name written all
over it.

5 = always, 4 = often, 3 = sometimes,
2 = rarely,   1 = never

1. I can make decisions without taking "analysis to the point of
    paralysis."

    5   4   3   2   1

2. I am willing to sacrifice some of my personal time to work the
    long hours success requires.

    5   4   3   2   1

3. I understand that customers are the source of my business,
    and I try to meet their needs to the best of my ability.

    5   4   3   2   1

4. I can take chances and trust my instincts without acting
    recklessly.

    5   4   3   2   1

5. I am not satisfied with past successes but continuously strive
    to reach new goals.

    5   4   3   2   1

6. Even if I am employed by someone else, I understand that I
    work for myself and take responsibility for my own success.

    5   4   3   2   1

Your total: _____

Your final score: Add your score for each question to get your final score. If you scored:

From 25 to 30 points: You and Lillian Vernon may be cut from the same cloth. If you are ever tempted to lower your standards of performance or service, remember that your commitment to excellence brought you this far and will ensure your continued success.

From 18 to 25 points: You do well enough until the going gets tough. Remember that success isn't all fun and games. Choose several success role models to inspire you, and make their stories part of your routine reading. Motivate yourself by writing down what others expect of you and what you expect of yourself, and review your list regularly.

Below 18 points: You aren't sure what you want or how to get it. Polish your customer service skills by putting buyers before yourself, and identify things that motivate you to take risks and work hard. Set goals for yourself with your manager, and remember that you have only a limited time to achieve the things you want. Start a collection of self-improvement materials to help you get serious about success.

EXECUTIVE DECISION

To this day the Lillian Vernon Corporation reflects this bullish adherence to the entrepreneurial spirit. The decision-making process is relatively simple. Get the facts, act on your best judgment, then acknowledge and correct any mistakes. Vernon feels that if she has hired and trained the right people to make good decisions, as the company president she has to let their decisions stand without interference from above.

"In the beginning," she says, "I felt like I was sacrificing my career, but it made sense. I encouraged my staff to act on the good instincts I hired them for and keep me posted on their activities. There's nobody to second guess their decisions or filter information before it reaches my desk. That also means there's nobody to cover up their mistakes. Entrepreneurs must stand or fall on their decisions, and if one of my employees cannot do that, we must part company."

Although Vernon admits that her management theory may not be so revolutionary as to outdo legendary Peter Drucker, it has led her through uncharted waters and brought unimaginable success. Since 1970, the Lillian Vernon Corporation has grown from two catalogs to five (including one specializing in children's merchandise called *Lilly's Kids*), has helped open the Chinese market as a product source, has built a national distribution center in Virginia Beach, and has become a publicly traded corporation—the only company on the American Stock Exchange founded by a woman.

What does the future hold for Lillian Vernon? More of the same groundbreaking adventures in untested and untapped direct markets. Lillian Vernon products have appeared on the QVC Shopping Network. It seems that her true-blue entrepreneurial heart keeps Lillian Vernon driven to create happy customers and keep the competition on the ropes.

"I take chances," she says, "by acting on my 'golden gut.' I try to keep the catalog creative and give my customers the proverbial offer they can't refuse. And most important, I know everything that is going on. There's nothing I hate more than waking up to find that one of my competitors is already doing something that I was planning on. That plus the ability to do things for other people and the opportunity to run a company with high standards of integrity and morality are the motivating factors that keep me going."

ACTION PLAN

- Make time for yourself and your family.
- Surround yourself with the best people possible.
- Be open to new ideas and better ways to do things.
- Don't dwell on your mistakes or setbacks—learn and grow from them.
- Don't grow without the proper systems and people in place.
- Be prepared to take risks.
- Like what you do and like what you sell.
- Don't try to do it all—delegate.
- Don't be afraid of technology that can make your business more efficient.
- Don't spend more money than you have—set realistic budgets and stick to them. Keep your debts manageable.

CHAPTER 4

HARVEY MACKAY

*The supersales pro from Minnesota tells the inside
story of his biggest sale.*

IT IS EASY TO LIKE and remember Harvey Mackay.
Long after you've listened to one of his speeches, and
long after you've read his book, his sleek one-liners continue to cruise your mind. "He who burns his bridges better be a damn good swimmer." Or "It isn't the people you
fire who make your life miserable; it's the people you
don't." Or "Find something you
love to do and you'll never have
to work a day in your life."

Harvey Mackay, owner and
CEO of the prosperous Mackay
Envelope Corporation in
Minneapolis, is a supersales pro.
He played a major role in per-
suading 28 NFL owners to bring

Fascinating Fact

*Mackay Envelope
boasts 500 employees
and produces
23 million envelopes
each day.*

the Super Bowl to Minneapolis in 1992, he was a catalyst in getting the $100 million Hubert H. Humphrey Metrodome sports complex built in Minneapolis, and he also wrote an international best seller that made publishing history.

 ACHIEVEMENT LESSONS

- **Hungry fighters don't tolerate complacency.** Always have your antenna up. Realize that complacency can happen to every single human being. Hungry fighters go to school for a lifetime. We need to use tapes, videos, books, and professional magazines to grow. If you don't grow, you die. It's like swimming across a lake. As long as you keep swimming, there is no problem, but as soon as you stop, you're going to go under.

- **Good leadership stretches people.** A good leader understands that anything that has been done a particular way for a given amount of time is being done the wrong way. Every single performance can be improved. Look at the field of sports. During the past 20 years every score has improved, regardless of the type of sport. The runners ran faster, the golfing scores went down, the bowling scores went up, high jumpers added inches, tennis balls went faster over the nets, swimmers crossed the finish line faster. Remember the old saying that even if you're on the right track, you'll get run over if you just sit there.

- **Wanting to be No. 1 shouldn't be your No. 1 goal.** I never wanted to be the largest envelope manufacturer in the United States. I decided to grow consistently over the past 30 years. I have a high respect for debt and don't want to get carried away by comparing the number of plants or the number of employees. My goal was to get the best return on investment, not to be No. 1. My mother, a schoolteacher, told me that there would always be somebody with a bigger car, a bigger house, a prettier girl on his arm, but that doesn't matter. Being No. 1 is often laughable. You have to measure yourself by your own standard of performance. You don't even want to try to keep up with the Joneses because every time you catch up with them, they refinance.

- **There is no substitute for perfect practice.** Practice doesn't make perfect. Perfect practice does. I am not a superior speaker, and I have been speaking for over 15 years, but when I prepared for my book promotions, I took voice lessons to improve my delivery. My voice teacher showed me how to breathe, how to use my voice, how to harness my energy, how to speak without getting hoarse. I am still taking more lessons; I am reading more books on voice training. It is hard work, but there is no substitute for perfect practice. There is also no substitute for the tremendous rewards.

- **Find out what you really want to do.** We all have goals, dreams, and desires. It's not easy to pin down what you really and truly want out of life. Start writing your dreams and goals on paper. Pale ink is better than the most retentive memory. Then develop identifiable, measurable, and attainable goals. Find something that you love to do and you'll never have to work a day in your life.

- **The greatest rewards come from helping other people.** My whole philosophy of life is based on personal relationships. That's how I built my company. That's how we got the Super Bowl to Minneapolis. That's how we raised money to build the Metrodome Stadium. One fourth of my time is devoted to volunteerism. I don't do things for people because they can help me. I've raised tens of millions of dollars for all kinds of causes across America, and I don't ever expect one thank-you note. If I expected it, then I'd be in deep trouble and shouldn't be a volunteer. I get the tremendous benefit that comes from the great feeling of helping another person.

His book *Swim With the Sharks Without Being Eaten Alive*, published in 1988, was rated the No. 1 business book in the United States, translated into some 16 languages, and distributed in 80 countries. As a result, demand for Mackay—already a popular speaker at major universities like Harvard and Stanford—skyrocketed, making him one of the highest paid speakers in the world today.

The bottom line? After he received a six-figure advance for the hardcover rights, the paperback rights were sold for a whopping $787,500.

When asked how he felt about his chances for producing another best seller, he responded with a smile: "After a hit, many people lose their intensity, their focus, or they simply stop being as hungry as they were before they wrote the big best seller. I take pride in challenging myself. I'm a hungry fighter."

SELLING A BEST SELLER

Mackay believes in doing his homework. Before he even wrote his first word, he interviewed more than 100 authors, publishers, agents, lawyers, and book sellers. In the process he slowly realized the many obstacles to getting his book published. Harvey explains that publishers receive about 500,000 manuscripts each year, but only 50,000 books get published. That makes the odds of getting published 1 in 10. Once

> **Fascinating Fact**
>
> *Swim With the Sharks Without Being Eaten Alive* spent 54 weeks on the New York Times' best-seller list.

a book is published, the odds of selling the publisher's initial press run of 10,000 books are even lower than that.

During his research Mackay learned that selling books is the only retail business in which the merchandise is sold on consignment. The standard industry expression is "gone today and here tomorrow." Unsold books are returned to the publisher's warehouse and then resold at deep discounts. He soon learned that creating a best seller would be a formidable challenge. Harvey Mackay's creative efforts for meeting this challenge and making it to the *New York Times'* best-seller list for more than 52 weeks in a row provide a unique study in marketing, selling, and Midwestern chutzpah:

> I had to create both an awareness of my book and some competition for it. Fortunately, I was able to talk to a publishing expert who arranged for me to appear live at the Stanford Publishing Program. My manuscript was compulsory reading for a class, and I got a unique chance to constructively change the book. At the same time, this session created an opportunity to evaluate my potential for marketing the book.

SELLING THE PUBLISHER

After this eye-opening experience, Mackay went back to the drawing board. He rewrote, polished, and edited his manuscript. Best-selling author Ken Blanchard (*The One Minute Manager*) arranged a meeting with Larry Hughes, publisher of William Morrow in New York:

> Hughes has a very big and very impressive corner office on Madison Avenue. He also had a key question for me. "What's

so different about your book?" I told him that I had visited at least 100 bookstores and studied the retail business.

When you walk into a store, you only look at the front covers of the books on display. You see 10 pictures of Iacocca, 10 pictures of Trump. Then I took him to the corner window and asked, "You see the tops of these trucks? For the past 27 years we have been painting our name, Mackay Envelope Corporation, on the tops of all our trucks which crisscross the United States. There is no significant price difference whether you have two panels or three panels painted."

Then I told him to use the same philosophy for selling my book. What's wrong with turning the book around and using the back cover for selling the book? The idea was to use the headline "You Can Judge This Book by Its Back Cover," and display the book twice, the first display showing the front cover, the second display showing the back cover. That way we'd double our chances for selling the book.

GETTING ENDORSEMENTS

The publisher was impressed with Mackay's sales and marketing insights. Later, he was even more impressed when Mackay came back with endorsements from such diverse figures as Ted Koppel, Billy Graham, Gloria Steinem, Walter Mondale, and Robert Redford. After a brief negotiation, he agreed to a six-figure advance, a $150,000 advertising and promotion budget, and a 100,000-copy first printing. An extraordinarily attractive deal for a first-time author. But how did Mackay get the celebrity endorsements?

The most important word in the English language, if you want to be a success, can't be found in the dictionary. It's "Rolodex."

Fascinating Fact

Mackay is a former No. 1 ranked tennis player in Minnesota.

I took 48 names and sent these people copies of my book with a nice cover letter. I've met most of these people at one time or another and worked at building the relationship. For example, Ted Koppel came one day to speak at the University of Minnesota. I picked him up at the airport. I knew about his passion for playing tennis, and he happened to be traveling with his tennis racket that day. He thought that there was enough time for hitting a few balls before his speech, and we headed for the tennis courts. We had a great time and then raced back to the meeting, with no time to spare. A few days later, I sent him a huge, seven-foot-long, 25-pound tennis racket with an oversize tennis ball and a small poem: "Here's to the Star of *Nightline*, To help him improve his sightline. Just line up the ball and then whack it, You'll never miss one with this racket." Ted Koppel sent a note back recommending that I give up poetry. He later sent this endorsement of my book: "Harvey Mackay takes you on an easy reader ride to success in the business world."

DEALING WITH REJECTION

Mackay's contract read that the book title had to be mutually agreeable to both the author and the publisher. William Morrow wanted a different title than *Swim With the Sharks Without Being Eaten Alive*. They told Mackay that the title was too long, that it didn't tell the reader what the book was about, and that some people might think that it was a book about skin diving. After a meeting with the publisher, Mackay's title was voted down 11 to 1. He went back to Minneapolis to rethink his strategy:

> Well, being reasonable, I had to accept the remote possibility that 11 professionals who run one of the most successful publishing houses in America might have a better idea of what would sell in the marketplace. But I wasn't ready to accept it yet. So I went to a local marketing research firm known for their expertise in creating and testing product names for companies like 3M, General Mills, or Procter & Gamble. They took 10 people who didn't know anything about business books. They worked on the book title for six hours. During the first hour they had to read about 50 pages of my book. They did not know my title. Their task was to find a title for my business book. After a few hours, they had 800 book titles pasted on the wall of the conference room. Interestingly, one of the titles was *Swim With the Sharks Without Being Eaten Alive*, which someone picked up from a sentence in the text. Then they began to put colored stars next to the titles they liked. *Swim With the Sharks*...received the most gold stars. Armed with this research, I went back to the publisher, and when I left, the vote was 12 to 0 in favor of *Swim With the Sharks*.

SELLING TO THE TOP

In any sales campaign, timing is crucial. The promotion for a book is no different. Harvey learned from publishing experts that the window of opportunity for making the best-seller list consists of a brief, six-week time span immediately following publication. All efforts—advertising, direct mail, media appearances, print interviews, book excerpts in magazines— have to be orchestrated with the precision of a Swiss watch:

> You have to remember that there are 50,000 titles published every year. Every time a book hits the shelves, these are 49,999 titles right behind it, ready to shove it off the shelves, right into the remainder bin. We squeezed a 15-city media tour into a 10-day blur. Publicity included excerpts in the airline magazines, the *Harvard Business Review,* and the *Los Angeles Times* with syndication in 40 newspapers across the country. Before the launch, I realized that Waldenbooks, the largest bookselling chain in the country [at that time], had ordered only 3,000 books. B. Dalton ordered the same quantity. That meant that *Sharks* would go belly-up before it barely made a splash.
>
> I went to Stamford, Connecticut, to see Harry Hoffman, chairman of Waldenbooks and one of the most powerful people in publishing and retailing. It's like going to Mecca, the place is kind of off-limits to authors, and that was all the more reason to go. I told Mr. Hoffman that I was scheduled to go on a 35-city tour and showed him the schedule of 125 radio and TV talk shows across the nation. Once he saw my single-mindedness and commitment, his order went from 3,000 to 15,000 hardcover books. A few days later, B. Dalton did the same. The archrival across the street had upped the ante.

SELLING AT EVERY LEVEL

At this point, Mackay was ready to sell his book through media appearances. It is estimated that after Mackay appeared on *Oprah* (with up to 16 million viewers), well over 35,000 consumers headed for the bookstores to buy *Swim With the Sharks*. Before the dizzying media tour began, Harvey launched a double-punch sales campaign that no author before him ever had conceived:

> We developed a special mailing to 5,000 bookstore managers in advance of the inventory shipment of my book. The envelope was manufactured by our company; it had a nice little gold seal and a bright red shark. The letter outlined the sales strategy, and it contained the endorsements and excerpts from the book and other selling information. I had the publisher's salespeople add a touch of class to the mailing with personalized notes. Then I made a stop at Ingram Books in Nashville, Tennessee. Ingram is the country's largest book wholesaler. After meeting with the president, I met with their telephone salespeople who are in touch with those 5,000 bookstores across the country. I gave each a copy of my book and a golden shark pin.
>
> They found out that I was a human being, and I found out that these people seldom see an author. So when any of the 5,000 bookstores calls them up and orders 27 Iacoccas and 40 Trumps, they may say, "Oh, incidentally, we've got *Swim With the Sharks*. . . . Do you want to try 30 of those?" The selling lesson? Little things mean a lot. Not true. Little things mean everything!

THE BIG PAYOFF

Harvey's book made it to the best-seller list within the first two weeks of publication. His strategy of doing his homework paid off. William Morrow knew that they had a hit on

To swim with the sharks and stay afloat, **BENCHMARKING** you need more than a life preserver. Arm yourself with innovation, testimonials, and a commitment to success, and take Harvey Mackay's other suggestions to work yourself into a selling frenzy. Take this quiz to see if you have the skills to keep your head above water, and, what to do if your score is less than perfect.

5 = always, 4 = often, 3 = sometimes,
2 = rarely,   1 = never

1. I believe in myself and my ability to succeed even where others have failed.

    5   4   3   2   1

2. I regularly collect testimonials from happy customers and use them in my presentations and promotions.

    5   4   3   2   1

3. I know the value of good business contacts and strive to meet new people and strengthen my current relationships.

    5   4   3   2   1

4. I pay attention to detail in my actions, appearance, written work, and in other areas that reflect on me.

    5   4   3   2   1

5. I am willing to do the legwork—making phone and face-to-face calls, staying in the trenches—to earn new customers.

    5   4   3   2   1

6. I try to differentiate my products and myself with creative thinking and innovative ideas.

    5   4   3   2   1

Your total: _____

Your final score: Add your score for each question to get your final score. If you scored:

From 25 to 30 points: You are a strong swimmer—just don't rest on your laurels. "After a hit," says Mackay, "many people lose their intensity," but you can maintain yours the way he does—by constantly challenging yourself.

From 18 to 24 points: To achieve success, commit to it. Ask yourself if you will put in the hours, do the legwork, and take care of the details—in other words, do the things that turn dreams of achievement into reality. To boost your momentum, set realistic goals and monitor your progress.

Below 18 points: Reevaluate your actions and your attitude. Build your confidence by improving your self-talk—remember that some of history's biggest successes were once failures too. Your brain is your best sales tool, so use it to think of novel ways to prospect or sell.

their hands and organized an auction to sell the paperback rights to Harvey's follow-up book.

"One day the president of William Morrow called to tell me about the auction. I asked, 'How many bidders will be there?' He said, 'About six.' I said, 'I'd like to meet them before they bid.' He replied, 'You can't do that, it's never been done before.' I told him, 'You didn't read my book. I don't want those people buying from a computer print-out. I want them to see me in the flesh. I want them to see commitment. I want them to hopefully see excellence, and perhaps they will think twice about it.' Within a matter of days, we sold the paperback rights for $787,500 to Fawcett. This was one of the largest paperback sales of a business book. Within weeks it catapulted to No. 1 on the

New York Times' best-seller list." While most people can think of a hundred different things they would do once they're successful, Mackay thinks of a hundred different action steps that lead to success.

"I did a hundred little things right—the title, the subtitle, the graphics, the endorsements, the rewriting, the direct mail, the personal visits, the hundreds of phone calls, the research, the media blitz, the sales strategy, all on top of the small job of writing a good book in the first place."

Mackay was so convinced that his book would make it that he even persuaded his publisher to offer a complete money-back guarantee to every consumer. Of the 600,000 hardcover copies sold, fewer than a dozen were returned.

The sales lesson: "Believe in yourself, even when nobody else does."

ACTION PLAN

- Defy the odds. Mackay didn't let the long odds of writing and publishing a best-seller deter him. Even when you think the biggest prospects, the biggest goals are beyond your reach, don't give up. When the tide turns against you, what can you do every day to maintain a good attitude and a good effort?

- Polish and revise your sales strategy. When he found out the first draft of *Swim With the Sharks* didn't measure up, Mackay edited and revised his work. To continuously improve your sales, continuously refine and improve your skills. How can you make small improvements to even your time-tested strategies?

- Do the little things well. The gold seal and red shark on Mackay's envelopes are little details that make a big difference. Taking care of such small details as sending greeting cards on special occasions or handling problems personally can help you retain buyers. What details do you overlook and how can you take care of them to exceed customer expectations?

CHAPTER 5

LARRY KING

CNN's talk show host with the most tells how to get buyers talking and bounce back to the top after you hit rock bottom.

L ARRY KING'S BROADCASTING mentor had the word "Salesman" after occupation on his driver's license. King neither peddles policies nor calls on accounts, but he has created a phenomenal success by building rapport while selling people on opening up to him in front of millions of listeners and viewers. From his early days in radio, broadcasting from a hotel lobby in Miami, his reputation has grown until he is now considered one of the giants of communication—with a big "C." Honored by professional societies, feted by celebrities, and courted by posh resorts, he

Fascinating Fact

Larry King was born Lawrence Harvey Zeiger on November 19, 1933.

nevertheless remains unabashedly excited about what he does best—getting people to talk.

Someone once said that success in convincing a person to buy your product is a matter of doing a thorough job of selling yourself first. If you accept that premise, then you must also admit that Larry King, in his own language, is one helluva sales pro. Guest after guest, night after night, month after month, year after year, King has been a consummate professional who knows how to get, and keep, the prospect's attention.

CURIOUS LARRY

From the time Larry King was eight years old, he has wanted to talk—and listen—to people. His natural curiosity about people's vocations, avocations, experiences, feelings, and talents has been boundless. One can easily imagine little Larry, standing beside his mother at the butcher shop, peppering the man in the white apron behind the counter with questions like, "Why rib roast? What's it like being a butcher? Do women come in here and tell you their problems? Didja ever want to go into vegetables?"

Fascinating Fact

At the last minute, King escaped military service during the Korean War because of poor vision in one eye.

King, who is listed in *The Guinness World Records* as having logged more hours on national radio than any other talk show host, estimates that he has interviewed more than 40,000 people. Numbers, however, do not begin to tell the Larry King story of success. Because King—and the name suits—is above all an interviewer who draws people to him while drawing them out. How can one explain why celebrities, politicians, authors, presidents and ex-presidents, athletes, and performing artists all feel comfortable and amiable sitting in front of this gregarious and articulate inquisitor? The most important quality—above and beyond talent, experience, insight, and all the rest—appears to be that King is always, on camera or off, natural. He knows who he is, what his weaknesses are, and where his strengths lie. He never deviates from what makes him comfortable. He is always himself.

As a kid I had an innate curiosity and a love of broadcasting. I always wanted to get into it, first radio, then television. And I was the kind of kid who interviewed everybody I met: "Why do you drive a bus? What's good about being a cop?" So I'm just extending what I always did. I always thought I would go into sports broadcasting, but in retrospect interviewing comes naturally to me. On radio and television, the producers book the guests so I talk to whoever shows up. Since I'm curious about everything, it doesn't matter to me who sits in that chair. In fact, I am very easy to book for. I'm more comfortable ad libbing than if I had something to read. I never read the books people are plugging. If I did, the questions wouldn't be fresh. I'd already know the answers and we'd have to talk about something else.

Getting people to open up is an art that Larry King has mastered. From such press-shy legendary greats as Frank Sinatra to master motivator Zig Ziglar, King elicits the same open confidence and camaraderie. Certain skills, which King claims are absolutely essential to one-on-one rapport, are easily transferable to other professional situations in which rapport can be the deciding factor in a make-or-break pitch. Number 1 is the attitude that King carries into all his interviews—he's impartial. Number 2 is that the guest rates priority No. 1 in any close encounter of the King kind. King never prejudges the guest's point of view. He has no ax to grind or buried bones to unearth. He is committed to letting the guest's light shine.

 ## ACHIEVEMENT LESSONS

He reigns supreme over today's talk realm, but Larry King has seen his share of trouble. Still, financial woes and even a heart attack couldn't keep him down. To make sure setbacks don't stop you either, learn these lessons from Larry.

- **Expect to make mistakes.** "Famous people can screw up and so can the host," says King—and so can you. On the fast track to the top, you can expect to stumble now and then. Be prepared for setbacks and you won't be as shaken by them.
- **Learn from the error.** After King went bankrupt, he paid someone else to manage his money. After his heart attack, he quit smoking and changed his diet. Mistakes can be helpful when they effect positive change. Ask yourself what you can learn from your blunders and what you can change to keep them from recurring.
- **Keep taking your chances.** King says that good communicators take risks; risk taking helps salespeople reach new heights as well. Guard against letting disappointments keep you inside your comfort zone. Instead, assess what you stand to gain and lose, and take risks without being reckless.

There isn't a soul who won't talk to you if you are sincerely interested in that person. But you have to create that empathy. The way you do that is you walk in their shoes a little and then you try to find out what those shoes are like. What is it like to step on a stage? What is it like to be known by everybody? What is it like to run a company? Now there is no chief executive officer who doesn't like to tell you about that. You could just as well say, "Your company lost a lot of money last year—what the hell's wrong?" But confrontation never works for me. Now you always have to do what works for you. What works for me is a little naiveté—innocence—even though it is obvious that I know what is going on in the world. Even if I have a guest on the show whose views are contrary to mine—he's the guest.

TO BANKRUPTCY AND BACK

It is well known that Larry King has had financial troubles in the past. Even while he was a successful radio show host in Miami, money slipped through his fingers or into bad investments, and, in 1973, he declared personal bankruptcy. In his book *Tell It to the King* (Larry King with Peter Occhiogrosso, Putnam, New York, 1988), he recalls that time. In his pocket he had the remaining half of a roundtrip plane ticket from Miami to Los Angeles where he had gone to seek work at any radio or TV station that would have him. The

Fascinating Fact

Larry Zeiger became Larry King on May 1, 1957, when he went on the air for the first time on Miami's WAHR radio.

trip was a washout, and on the last day, with a scant $3 in his pocket, he stopped his rental car (in those days, as King recalls, you could still rent a car for cash at the airport) at the Beverly Hills Hotel, walked the flight down to the coffee shop, and ordered a milkshake to fill up his empty stomach. The check came to $3, and King was chagrined at not being able to dole out a tip to the countergirl. To get his car from valet parking, he made up a story about leaving his wallet behind in his hotel room. He then drove straight to the airport, used the same line at the car rental return and told them to bill him, then approached a friendly looking fellow in the airport terminal and asked to borrow some money for newspapers to read on the plane. The man gave him $5 and told him to get a bite to eat, and King arrived back in Miami completely broke and still unemployed.

Fourteen years later, Larry King, now famous and successful, arrived at the eighth annual Ace Awards, cable television's highest honor, where he would emcee (for which he was paid $5,000) and where he would also receive the award for best talk show host. He arrived escorted by Angie Dickinson in her Mercedes, and they pulled up to the Beverly Hills Hotel where the luncheon was to be held. Flash bulbs popped, the press crushed toward them, and King found himself on the same stairs leading to the coffee shop, where milkshakes were now $4. Dazed for the moment, he looked around and felt strange and at the same time extremely proud. Six weeks later he had a heart attack that resulted in multiple bypass surgery and a new way of life for King.

My book is about famous people who put their pants on one leg at a time. Famous people can screw up, and so can the host. In my case, the two greatest failings were also the two best things that happened for me. Financial failure and heart failure. I couldn't handle money. If I hadn't gotten knocked down, I would have continued borrowing from Peter to pay Paul. I would still be in Miami making $70,000 and spending $90,000. But I got shut down so bad that when I came back, I put the money in other people's hands to manage for me. I have no idea what a CNN or Mutual Broadcasting paycheck looks like. The money all goes to Boston where I pay the management firm $113,000 a year to manage my money. In 1983 I wasn't even making that much in a year. I got real lucky. The CNN show took off. But now I'm still living like I was in 1983 when I was making $100,000 a year and paying the manager in Boston $10,000. It's fine. I have a company Lincoln Continental, I fly first class, which is in my contract. When I land, there is a limo waiting. The rest is all invested for me. Now I can afford tips. On a recent trip to La Costa, I tipped $1,000 on a $4,200 bill. After I declared bankruptcy, I started all over again. I lived with my mother for a while. I got lucky and went right back on the radio and back to the newspaper. Within two years I had the television talk show. But most of my failures or disappointments were self-inflicted. I can look back and say very few people wronged me. After the heart attack, I changed my lifestyle—no more smoking, I watch my diet now—I lost weight. I have been lucky enough to survive both calamities and come back to feel terrific. I put my financial house in order only because I take care of myself and other people take care of my money for me.

LARRY KING LIVE

Larry King's expertise and charisma as an interviewer is matched by his presence in front of an audience. He delights in holding them in the palm of his hand, leading them to a punch line, developing the drama of a good yarn well spun. He never reads a speech, nor does he even know beforehand what particular story he may use to lay his audience in the aisles. All alone, he stands there, he has a sense of whom he is speaking to, and then he lets them have it. From a backlog of stories that goes back to his boyhood in Brooklyn and all the celebrities, politicians, comedians, speakers, and tycoons he has known since, he weaves the texture of talk that never fails to rivet the attention of his audience.

My biggest kick is making people laugh. Interviewing famous people and learning about them is wonderful. But when you can stand up in a room and hear a pin drop, control them and make them laugh, that is the high of all highs. I understand what great comedians go through. That feeling of power that you can go anywhere you want with them. When I would watch comics, before I started doing speeches, I would ask them how they could keep it fresh time after time. They said that every time is like the first time. There is a truism in that because sometimes you are even better because you are so heightened. A warmth develops between you and the audience. I would tell a story but I knew where the ending was but I was as heightened about reaching it as the audience was and I had told it 10 times before. I don't just think of the story on the spot, but I have no idea what stories I will tell or which way it will go when I am up there. A lot depends on the group. So there is a magic.

To the manor born in no way describes King's early life. His father died when Larry was 10. His mother had lost a son before Larry was born and then lost her own mother. Consequently she overindulged Larry and thought he could do no wrong. Life in Brooklyn was poor, and it meant street survival for a boy like Larry, which is perhaps why men like Mario Cuomo find in King a comrade in arms and a good friend. King never made the secret vow "When I grow up I'm going to make it big." Instead, he learned by trial and error that meaning comes before money, and the meaning is what keeps the work rich:

> After my father died, we were on welfare for a year. New York City bought my first pair of glasses. My mother spoiled me, and that was coupled with the fact that I was never taught much responsibility. On the other hand, she gave me a lot of love. She also gave me an ability to fall down and come up again. Then at 22 I started making $22,000 a year, reading my name in the *Miami Herald*, and I wanted to have that Cadillac. But in the beginning, as early as age 6, I wanted to get on the radio. I never had dreams of a national show. What do you do when reality exceeds your dreams— Albert Brooks says you shut up about it. You stay excited. You stay interested in what makes your guest tick whether you make $10,000 or $1 million. The money is a by-product. But in the early days I had too much too soon. Too much attention. I never defined success then. Today I would define it as doing what you want.

SMOOTH TALKER

In an age when communication has become a catchall phrase for everything from selling political ideologies to

Larry King didn't grow up with big money **BENCHMARKING** or big connections, but he was a winner on the inside. To score your own self-made success, adopt the qualities that helped him talk his way to the top, including curiosity, resilience, and empathy. Test yourself to find out if you and King share the same winning characteristics and, if not, how to make them part of you and your sales strategy.

5 = always, 4 = often, 3 = sometimes,
2 = rarely,   1 = never

1. I try to take a sincere interest in my customers' business problems and in their families and personal interests.

5   4   3   2   1

2. I understand my strengths and weaknesses, and I make the most of what I have while improving my shortcomings.

5   4   3   2   1

3. I try to understand what it's like to be my prospects, and I show empathy for their feelings and situation.

5   4   3   2   1

4. When I make a mistake, I look for the lesson in it and make positive changes as a result.

5   4   3   2   1

5. When buyers are on the fence about my product, I tell a convincing sales story to help them make up their minds.

5   4   3   2   1

6. I know taking risks helps me improve, and I'm not afraid to take a chance to earn a new customer.

5   4   3   2   1

Your total: _____

Your final score: Add your score for each question to get your final score. If you scored:

From 25 to 30 points: Sales records are yours for the breaking. Keep up the good work, and keep in mind the meaning of what you do and how it helps others. Someday you may find yourself talking to Larry King in an interview about your phenomenal success.

From 18 to 24 points: You may be losing sight of your buyers' individuality. Remember that they are people, first and foremost. Your curiosity about them and your ability to empathize with them and share stories with them tells them you understand that. Spend some extra time with buyers—take them to lunch or just call to make sure they are doing well.

Below 18 points: You probably don't share a strong bond with your buyers and seem easily discouraged by setbacks. Shift your focus from the business to the personal side of selling. When you take care of customers, the numbers may take care of themselves. When you make a mistake or get rejected, objectively analyze the causes, then move on.

---

pitching detergent, some super communicators shine like beacons from a lighthouse. Larry King's brief, choppy style keeps the guest and the audience moving along as if on an electric current. Sometimes we get a slight jolt, but more often, we feel the steady surge of juice and we don't want to turn off the switch:

> A good communicator communicates. There are no rules. I don't know why William Faulkner talked in endless sentences when he was a brilliant writer. Arthur Godfrey spoke in a monotone, if you judged his voice alone, but he was a great communicator. Red Barber had a severe Southern twang, yet he was

great in front of a mike. I am a basic New Yorker who can appeal to people in Biloxi. Good communicators take risks. Johnny Carson told me that, and it's true. Godfrey was a risk taker. I have nothing prepared before my show, and every night I am at risk. I never say to myself, "Is this a stupid question?" I risk saying, "I don't know." I risk going to my instincts and trusting them. I am never dishonest with the audience.

The qualities that have helped Larry King survive and thrive in broadcasting are just as useful off the air in one-on-one situations like sales. In fact, King has known some of the great sales pros of our time:

Gene Letterman, who wrote *The Sale Begins When the Customer Says No*, was fantastic; Harvey Mackay who wrote *Swim With the Sharks* was good. Also Herb Cohen, Zig Ziglar, Johnny Carson. You know the truest thing is you sell yourself. Arthur Godfrey was a great salesman. In fact, his driver's license said "Salesman." He once said to me, "That's all we are, Larry. I'm just honest enough to put it down."

ACTION PLAN

- Create empathy. By putting himself in his guests' shoes, King encourages them to open up to him. To earn your buyers' trust, try to understand what their jobs are like, what pressures and problems they face, and how they view you. What can you do to learn more about your buyers and show them you understand them and their situations?

- Treat prospects with equal courtesy and respect. To bond with guests, King sets his opinion aside and approaches interviews impartially. Valuable prospects don't look, sound, or act according to a set formula, so don't prejudge them. How can you stop stereotyping or labeling people and give them all the same courteous, attentive treatment?

- Tell a tale. King holds audiences spellbound with stories of his boyhood, guests, and famous acquaintances. Good stories—especially of someone in circumstances similar to your prospect's—help illustrate your main points, convincing the listener to buy. How can you work more true sales stories into your presentation?

PART II

FACE-TO-FACE: INTERVIEWS WITH THE MASTERS

CHAPTER 6

ZIG ZIGLAR

*The motivational guru shows how a positive attitude
can change your life.*

IT IS EASY to be motivated by Zig Ziglar. His tone of voice alone communicates the message that attitude is the key to success in life. His whole being is a study of motivation in action.

He is a person with a strong, well-established guiding philosophy, one that has something of enduring value for everyone. He expresses it with the words, "You can get everything in life you want, if you help enough other people get what they want."

This maxim is certainly true in selling, but it is equally true in any other field. By helping others, you help yourself. We live in a world of interdependence and mutuality.

If one is to learn from Zig about becoming a super-achiever, one must listen to him intently and then put into practice what he presents. Knowledge increases with repeated practice. Many people have turned their lives around because they decided to apply Zig's principles to improve their lives.

An impeccable person to deal with, Zig Ziglar's foundation reflects integrity and inner strength. He is convinced that we have a profound effect on one another and that it is important to make positive contacts to get positive results.

The age-old question of whether the glass is half full or half empty is still with us. The only change is that today we are lucky enough to have Zig Ziglar to help us see the glass waiting to be filled to the brim, by us. If you follow Zig's guiding philosophy, your glass will never again be half empty.

Ziglar's electrifying speeches have a reputation for drawing long-standing ovations and leaving audiences spellbound.

He is his own best success story. It began in Yazoo City, Mississippi. He was born one of 12 children. His father died when he was five, leaving his mother with five kids too young to work.

He became one of the most successful cookware sales pros of all time, but he quit knocking on doors when he recognized his charisma for motivating others.

Although Zig has been interviewed by many reporters (including Morley Safer of *60 Minutes*), this exclusive interview explores new answers to the familiar question facing salespeople in today's economy: "What can I do to motivate myself?"

Question: In one of your speeches you mentioned that negative thinking is as common as the cold. Did you find a cure for negative thinking?

Ziglar: If you feed your mind with positive thoughts, if you are selective about the things that you choose to read, look at, or listen to, then you are taking effective action against negative thinking. It's just like with a computer; if you change the input, you will change the output.

Question: So you are saying that there is a direct link between negative thinking and negative input and that people can become more selective about the input?

Ziglar: Absolutely. Let me give you an example. Thomas M. Hartman from Oklahoma City weighed 407 pounds when he attended a rally. He had just gone through a devastating divorce; he was floating checks so he could eat from one week to the next; he held a job only because his boss was a friend, not because he was productive. During our all-day seminar he began to think that he could do something. He got a set of my tapes, *How to Stay Motivated*, and started listening. He told me he has heard that set more than 500 times. He could quote me verbatim from start to finish. Today, Tom weighs 200 pounds; he's happily remarried; he teaches a Sunday school class every week. He has graduated magna cum laude in psychology and is working toward his doctorate. He's in business for himself.

Question: It sounds like your positive input has helped him to lead a more successful life. What is your definition of success?

Ziglar: I believe that you're successful when you've dealt with the physical, the mental, and the spiritual self successfully. If I made millions and destroyed my health in the process, or if I become the best at what I do but neglect my family, I wouldn't call that success.

Question: One of your claims is that your attitudes in life determine ultimately how successful you become.

Ziglar: Yes. Dr. William James has said the most important discovery of our time is the realization that by altering our attitudes, we can alter our lives. There is also a Harvard University study that points out that 85 percent of the reason people are hired or get ahead in their jobs is directly related to their attitudes.

Question: What is your theory of self-motivation? How do you develop it?

Ziglar: From time to time, in some egghead discussions with my intellectual friends, I'm told that all motivation is self-motivation. I respond to that in *See You at the Top* with a little analogy. When I build a fire in my fireplace, it will burn for a while. Then I notice that there are no flames. It has died down. I get up and take my poker and shake up those logs. All of a sudden, we've got bright flames. Now, all I did was just poke them, which created some motion. The motion creates a partial vacuum, and new air is pulled into the fireplace. With an additional supply of oxygen, the fire ignites, and now we've got a flame. If I hadn't done some poking, there would have been no flame.

Now, this business about all motivation being self-motivation is only partially true. You can choose among many different sources to rekindle your motivation. In other words, the environment you select and the people you associate with become large contributing factors.

Question: Positive relationships will contribute to positive motivation?

Ziglar: Certainly. One day I heard my son saying, "The thing I like best about my Dad is that he loves Mom." You see, positive relationships create a feeling of closeness and become a source of strength. The likelihood of motivating yourself is greatly increased with positive relationships.

The equation also works the other way. I've been active in the war against drugs for a long time. I strongly believe that a person is inclined to use dope in direct proportion to the number of times it is offered to him or her.

Question: And to the frustrations that he or she is carrying around without knowing how to deal with them.

Ziglar: Yes, he or she might say no 17 times, but then that one day comes when he or she has had a bad day and feels frustrated and exasperated, and is unable to recognize the danger and is bound to suffer in the long run.

Question: Do you feel that the exclusive focus on the positive side of life can lead to a new set of problems?

Ziglar: There is always a possibility. I do believe, though, that if you were to take 100 cases, you'd find 95 times that the positive response is going to be the right approach.

Question: So the positive input and the positive attitude need to be supplemented with a sound business plan and professional skills.

Ziglar: Absolutely. Let me sum it up this way. Positive thinking is an optimistic hope, not necessarily based on any facts. Positive believing is the same optimistic hope, but this time based on a sound reason.

Question: I've heard many sales managers express doubts about the value of a motivational seminar. They say, "Our people get fired up for a while and they are totally enthusiastic, but two days later they're back in the same old groove—nothing changed."

Ziglar: Well, let me refer to it indirectly. Another reporter once asked in a different way the same question. He said, "The charge is that motivation is not permanent. How do you respond to that?" And I said, "Absolutely right!" It is not permanent. Neither is bathing. But if you bathe every day, you're going to smell good. In my seminars I explain that 15 minutes a day of motivation from a good audio tape or a book can make a tremendous difference in your life and give you a motivational lift *every* day.

Question: You've said once that life is simple but not easy and that too many people are looking for quick and easy solutions.

Ziglar: Right.

Question: The answers that you give in your speeches and your tapes, are they simple and easy to apply?

Ziglar: Simple and easy to understand. But I'll never tell you life is easy. There are a lot of days when you don't feel like doing your job. But I firmly believe that the best work is often done by people who don't feel like doing it. You know, the mother wakes up at two o'clock in the morning, with her baby crying; she's had a tough night and a tough day, but she's gonna get up because of love and responsibility.

Question: You recommend that salespeople should listen to your tapes 16 times to completely absorb the full message?

Ziglar: Let me explain why I suggest they listen so many times. There are several university studies revealing that two weeks after you've learned anything new, unless it's reinforced, you remember only about 4 percent of it. That's the first reason. The second reason is that while we are listening, we may experience a certain mood, and our minds will seek out messages that relate to that particular mood. On another day, let's say you just made a sale; you'll be in a different mood, and a whole new range of messages of the same recording will become clear in your mind. So by listening 16 times, the odds are that you will have absorbed the entire content.

Question: Let's say I've listened 16 times to your tapes on motivation. Do I know then how to motivate myself?
Ziglar: Yes.

Question: Do I master the skills sufficiently so that I become independent of your tapes?
Ziglar: Only if you've been practicing the things we've been advocating. It's like driving a car. You don't learn to drive a car by watching someone else drive.

Question: Can I graduate in self-motivation, ever?
Ziglar: Boy, that's a tough one. Nobody has ever asked me that before. I don't think so, and I don't think I've graduated, because I constantly read and constantly study. I think you could draw an analogy with eating. You can't graduate in eating. You need to continue to make choices about your input. The same is true with self-motivation. You need to continue to make choices about what level of self-motivation you want to maintain.

Question: You seem to have an unusual ability to create persuasive analogies to illustrate your point. In your book See You at the Top, *you've used more than 800 analogies, one-liners, and power phrases. How did you develop this technique?*

Ziglar: Well, one of the things I did when I first got interested in motivation was to buy a yearly datebook, and on the top of every page there was a power phrase, a one-liner. So I started writing them down. This was long before the days of audio recordings. I wrote them on three-by-five cards, and I put them up on the visor of my car. And I'd be riding down the highway and thinking about them. Over the years, I committed to memory several hundred of them.

Question: Many salespeople have a tough time in this economy. What thoughts can you offer to approach these tough challenges more positively?

Ziglar: A good friend of mine, Calvin Hunt in Victoria, Texas, said, "You know, Zig, it's an absolute fact that when we are in an economic slump, 50 percent of all salespeople literally slow down rather than speed up their efforts. They are not motivated to do something. They lose that enthusiasm.

"Now," he continued, "when that happens, it simply means that if business is down 20 percent, but 50 percent of the salespeople are not nearly as active, your own personal prospect list is considerably higher than if there was no recession."

Question: And the winners still keep winning.

Ziglar: Absolutely. It's their discipline, their commitment to maintain a high level of motivation, and their sense of direction that gets them to the top.

ACTION PLAN

- We can't graduate in self-motivation. It's like eating. We can't graduate in eating. We need to continue to make choices about what level of self-motivation we want to maintain.
- The likelihood of motivating yourself is greatly increased with positive relationships. Positive relationships create a feeling of closeness and become a source of strength.
- If you feed your mind with positive thoughts, if you are selective about the things that you choose to read, look at, or listen to, then you are taking effective action against negative thinking.
- Success is not measured by what you've done compared to others but compared to what you're capable of doing.
- To succeed in selling, use emotion and logic in your sales presentation. Logic makes people think; emotion makes them act. If you use only logic, you'll end up with the best-educated prospect in town. If you use only emotion, you'll end up with a canceled order. Balance these keys and you'll sell more.

CHAPTER 7

MARY KAY ASH

*The queen of direct selling speaks on the importance
of self-fulfillment.*

"MOST PEOPLE PLAN their vacations better than they plan their lives," said Mary Kay Ash. But for the 170,000 salespeople in the Mary Kay organization, planning and goal setting are daily routine.

More women make more than $50,000 a year working for Mary Kay than in any other American company.

How do they do it? With enthusiasm, according to their mentor and the founder of this empire. She was America's No. 1 woman sales pro.

Mary Kay's own enthusiasm has spilled over into thousands upon thousands of lives, like waves on the shore. They wash over each other, breaking down the sands of silent despair and building the cliffs of hope from which each woman can see her own horizon.

Mary Kay, more than any other woman in business, represents a way for women to have their cake and eat it too. They have been able to fulfill their hopes and dreams while maintaining their dignity and an independence few had ever known before Mary Kay's company came into existence. Some who began their Mary Kay careers with the humblest of expectations have turned into top sales producers with six-figure incomes.

All of this is possible because of the guiding philosophy of the woman who started it all. Underlying the expression of enthusiasm, we see a woman who had a deep respect and understanding of her fellow women; their dreams were her dreams, their needs were also hers. At a time when women in sales were a rarity, Mary Kay was outperforming everyone. When she started her own company, against the advice of male experts, she made sure that she would never make the same assumptions about women that were made about her.

With this goal in mind, she created a structure that gives women recognition, respect, and rewards.

During the interview she recalled her mother's philosophy: "If you give a man a fish, you feed him for a day, but if you teach him how to fish, you feed him for life." Mary Kay translated this guideline to feed and nurture thousands of women.

The main objective of this philosophy is that others must be able to incorporate into their own lives what you have created through yours. What you create must improve those lives, and it must strengthen the bonds between people. This philosophy will go on nurturing and feeding women long after Mary Kay has gone.

Mary Kay's enthusiasm was always catching. The warmth she radiated was enveloping. To be in her presence made one feel happy to be alive and glowing with the possibilities of the moment. She provided the structure, she set the example, and she worked hard. But, most of all, she let you know, by all that she had done, that, "Honey, you can do it, too."

What Mary Kay created amounts to the unbelievable success story of America's most dynamic saleswoman. Sadly, the world lost this amazing business woman on November 22, 2001. This interview shares the basic principles that accounted for her inner growth and sales success.

Question: The first thing that strikes me about your organization is the incredible enthusiasm that is expressed by your staff and your consultants. How do you generate this enthusiasm?

Ash: Somebody said, if you act enthusiastic, you will become enthusiastic. We try to generate enthusiasm by example.

Question: What are some of the things you do to set the example?

Ash: One of the things that I do personally is to keep some very good books on my bedside table that keep reminding me of what life is really all about. There are some days when you wake up and you really don't feel all that enthusiastic. I think that is true of every person.

Question: It's true. What kind of books do you feel are helpful for those days?

Ash: Besides the Bible, there are some very good motivational books, like Norman Vincent Peale's *The Power of Positive Thinking*, or one that inspired me and turned my life around at one time, *Think and Grow Rich* by Napoleon

Hill; and of course *Psycho-Cybernetics* by Dr. Maxwell Maltz. All of these are not exactly the newest things on the market, but I keep reading the new ones and rereading the old ones. They keep me enthusiastic.

Question: How do you help your salespeople to maintain their enthusiastic attitude?

Ash: We have a lot to be enthusiastic about. But even back in those days when the success was small, we found ways to be enthusiastic about the things we did have. There are many ways to create enthusiasm in a group of salespeople. For example, we hold most sales meetings on Monday morning to challenge the "blue Monday syndrome." To me, Monday is a new beginning, a fresh start, and a new chance to do something positive. So, we start by singing songs. I feel very strongly about the effect of music and the action of singing. When you go to church, invariably the hymns are sung first. They create a very special feeling that leads to a positive attitude.

Question: You've said that the test of a champion is "to be able to put on a happy face when deep down you are suffering over a serious problem." No matter how bad you feel, you must always go in enthusiastically. When your hostess says, "Hello, how are you?" the consultant must respond, "Wonderful, and how are you?" Isn't that a form of self-denial?

Ash: No, I don't really think so. I think it has a therapeutic effect. For example, one of our directors, Rena Tarbet, has hit the Million Dollar Club for the third year. She has had cancer for seven years. Twenty-two days a month, she is on some kind of treatment that would normally put most of us in the hospital. Her doctor says, "Rena is living with cancer, not dying with it."

Just recently, one of her family-members called me and they thought she was working too hard—she is now working on her fourth million, it is incredible—and I called her doctor to get his views. He said, "It is my opinion that it is that incredible, indomitable spirit of hers that keeps her going, and that is why she is where she is today, and I think she should be allowed to do anything she feels like doing."

Question: Rena's work seems to prevent her from getting worse.

Ash: Right. You heard about the man who said, "If I only went to work on the days I felt like it, I never would." If Rena stayed home and focused on the fact that she is ill, she would probably get worse.

Question: Is it true that some of your salespeople start their workday at five o'clock in the morning?

Ash: It's true. You know, if you get up at five o'clock three times a week, you'll gain an extra day. You need to try it a few times because you'll realize a great feeling of satisfaction at eight o'clock in the morning when you've already finished what would have taken you six hours to do after eight o'clock because of the interruptions.

It's not infrequent that I get a call at five or six o'clock in the morning, and I always know that it is one of my eager beavers who is already up. An example is one of my top producers, Helen McVoy. She made $310,000 last year.

Question: So you feel you've had a head start while other people are still sleeping.

Ash: Yes. By the time they get out of their beds, you've already finished half a day's work.

Question: It seems that you learned to work hard at a very early age.

Ash: I think I probably had a different situation from the average child. I don't ever remember my mother's being there to bake cookies or do any of the things that most mothers do, or help me with my lessons and tie my shoes. She had the very inconvenient situation of being away from me, and I think perhaps she felt a little guilty about not being able to be there to do the things that she thought that she should be doing. So she used the telephone. You know that old saying, "If you give a man a fish, you feed him for a day, but if you teach him how to fish, you feed him for life." My mother applied that principle. Over the telephone, she would tell me exactly how to do every little thing that I needed to know as a child. She always would say, "Honey, you can do it," or "Anything anyone else can do, you can do better." I think that the reason she would constantly add "You can do it" was that she wasn't really sure I could.

Question: In a way, your mother's expectations seem to have translated into your expectations of your people in the Mary Kay organization where you encourage others by saying "You can do it too."

Ash: Right. That's what we do on a constant, everyday basis.

Question: It's a very powerful principle.

Ash: It worked for me. And it's working today for a lot of people. I am amazed at how many people come up to me and say, "You know, I met you in Chicago and you took my hand and you looked in my eyes and you said, 'You know, I just know that you can do it.'"

Question: Do you feel that women need to be motivated differently from men?

Ash: In some ways, I think men are motivated more by money than women are. I've often heard men say, "Why do you spend all this money on a mink coat? Why don't you just give them cash?" I don't think that women would be as motivated by cash as they would by the possibility of having a mink coat that they have dreamed about all their lives. If they received the cash, it probably would go for a dishwasher or something like that.

Question: What do you feel is the No. 1 motivator that women respond to?

Ash: Recognition comes first, self-fulfillment second, and then third, I think, is pride.

Question: Self-fulfillment would mean...

Ash: Accomplishing something that probably their husbands didn't think they could do or maybe they themselves didn't think they could do.

Question: In a way, you create a competitive situation that allows them to get recognized and feel fulfilled.

Ash: Well, we've created a competitive situation, but we've removed all the dog-eat-dog jealousy factor and all the scratching somebody else's eyes out to get where you want to go.

Question: What do you do to prevent that?

Ash: In some of the companies that I was in, there was always a first, second, and third prize, and invariably there were always three hot shots in the company who would win those. So what's the use of trying? We put everything on a plateau basis. In other words, if we have a contest, you know that it will take X number of dollars wholesale to get into that rank. You don't have to step on anybody to get the reward; you can all reach for it and get it. In essence, our salespeople compete with themselves.

Question: Do you feel that this system leads to a better over-all attitude among salespeople?

Ash: Absolutely. We are talking about creating a go–give attitude. If you give the very best you have in whatever you do, the best will then come back to you in a kind of boomerang effect. It certainly has worked for me, and the more I give, the more it comes back. And yet, you don't ever think about it. I mean, I never think about that when I am giving, I'm going to get a whole lot back. That doesn't work. You give without any expectation of return.

Question: You also suggest to put God first, family second, and career third.

Ash: Right. If you put God first in your life, you don't have to worry about much else. Then, your family should come next. It is my opinion that if you make the most money in the whole world and in the process lose your husband and your children just for the dollar, then you've failed.

Question: Life would lose its meaning.

Ash: Yes, there are a lot of things more important than just making money.

Question: Managing a family and a career calls for a certain amount of organizational skills and good time management habits.

Ash: Yes, it does.

Question: What are some success principles that you've developed for yourself in this area?

Ash: Well, one of the most important principles that I ever learned is to write each evening the six most important things I have to do tomorrow. I also number them in the order of their importance. You need to make that decision because a woman can walk into any room of the house and find six things that need to be done. By deciding what's most important, I can follow what I set out to do and don't get off on all kinds of tangents.

Question: Why 6 items and not 10 or 12?

Ash: You need to balance the number of tasks with your possibilities of completing them in the time available. If you would write down 26 items, you'd get frustrated and say, "I can't do all that," and you'd end up doing nothing. But 6 things you can do. And then I always say, with a smile, "If you get those done, you can take the rest of the day off with my blessing."

Question: Do you always begin to work with a clean desk in the morning?

Ash: I usually start with a clean desk.

Question: And when you finish the day?

Ash: I take it all home.

Question: The reading matter?

Ash: Oh, I have it in nice little piles here. One is to read, one is to sign, and one is for dictation. I like to work on these things early in the morning while I'm real fresh. There is another little habit that applies to time management and organization. I've discovered that whatever is on top of your incoming mail, you take it and finish it. I don't go on to the second, no matter how enticing. Normally you tend to go through the pile and think, "Oh, here is an easy one, I'll do that one first," and, "I don't know the answer to this one, so I'll put it aside for a while." My suggestion is: You tackle one thing at a time and finish it, no matter how difficult it is or how easy it is. You don't handle any piece of paper twice.

Question: Sooner or later you'll have to make the decision anyway. So it's better to make it now.
   Ash: Right, get it over with.

Question: Doesn't it feel good to cross things off your list?
   Ash: Yes, I love it.

Question: How do you deal with procrastination? I've heard that sometimes there is a little problem with follow-up calls.
   Ash: Yes. It is caused by fear of rejection when they think, "Oh, my goodness, that lady may not like it ... maybe I couldn't answer her question. Maybe she's not at home."

Question: Even though they may have the item on their list, this fear prevents them from completing the job.
   Ash: Yes.

Question: How do you suggest they deal with it?
   Ash: Well, by discipline first of all. I suggest that they put aside one hour, put a sand-timer in front of them, and talk to one person every three minutes. Make that call and succinctly ask the questions that need to be asked, do whatever has to be done, and get off the phone to call the next

person. Many consultants have a tendency to talk too long and talk for 35 minutes because they enjoy it. If she would keep these calls short and businesslike, she would keep her business in fine shape and would keep her bookings and her production going. Our top producers say that an ounce of pink tickets (follow-up call reminders) is worth an ounce of gold.

Question: You were once quoted as saying: "One intense hour is worth a dreamy day." What did you mean by that?

Ash: Well, Parkinson's law states that "work expands to fill the time available for it." If somebody called you from the airport saying, "We just arrived in town and we'll be there in half an hour," you'd get your spring cleaning done in 30 minutes, when you might have spent a whole day on it. Whatever length of time you have available for a project, like these follow-up calls, you get it done.

Question: So if you don't develop sound time management principles, you won't be able to reach your goals.

Ash: Right.

Question: What are some of the success principles you use that apply to goal setting?

Ash: Well, first of all, you're never going to get there if you don't know where you are going. I think most people plan their vacations better than they plan their lives.

Question: It sounds as if the success principles you've applied in your company since 1963 have helped you grow far beyond what you imagined you could do.

Ash: Well, I feel that God had a very important job to be done here. You know that I am a great-grandmother?

Question: Right.

Ash: So I realize that time is precious and that I don't have forever to do all these things. For this reason I am trying to set the concepts so that other Mary Kays can carry on long after I am gone.

Question: How do you think this will happen?

Ash: I think this will come about through my national sales directors, who, in essence, believe in everything I believe in, and who are where they are because they are almost stamped-out copies. I have just returned from a 10-day trip with the top 10 nationals. Just being with them every day was an interesting experience—it was almost like looking into a mirror.

Question: It appears that one of your greatest contributions to the expansion of your company was to motivate a large number of people to use their own capabilities and to apply many of your proven success principles.

Ash: Yes, I think that is really true. I think that one of the greatest contributions we have made is to help people realize how great they really are and to reach their potential.

ACTION PLAN

- If you give the very best you have in whatever you do, the best will come back to you in a boomerang effect.
- Write down each evening the six most important things you have to do the next day. By deciding what's most important, you can follow what you set out to do and not go off on tangents.
- If you get up at five o'clock three times a week, you'll gain an extra day. Try it, and you'll realize the great feeling of satisfaction at eight o'clock in the morning when you've already finished what would have taken you six hours to do after eight o'clock because of the interruptions.
- Don't handle any piece of paper twice. Whatever is on the top of your incoming mail, take it and finish it. Don't go on to the second, no matter how enticing.
- People plan their vacations better than they plan their lives.

CHAPTER 8

F. G. "BUCK" RODGERS

❧ ———— ❧

*Former IBM executive turned motivational
sales coach shares his philosophy for solution-
oriented selling.*

IF THERE'S ONE COMPANY that exemplifies successful selling in this century, it is the IBM Corporation.
One of the significant contributors to that success was F. G.
"Buck" Rodgers who began at the firm as a sales trainee
and ultimately became vice president of sales and marketing. Today Rodgers is a popular motivational speaker and
the best-selling author of *The IBM Way* and *Getting the Best
Out of Yourself and Others.*

Rodgers is a team player, the more so now that he is on
his own. He still promotes the concepts that have been so
successful at IBM. He speaks to university and business
audiences all over the country about what goes into the
making of an effective and efficient model of marketing and
management.

Rodgers believes the more complex and competitive our society has become, the more important it is for customers to feel their needs are recognized, their problems addressed, and workable solutions presented. Buck Rodgers exemplifies this solution-oriented approach to selling.

Fifty-six years ago, F. G. "Buck" Rodgers began what turned out to be an illustrious career with the then-smallish (sales of $250 million) IBM Corporation. The year was 1950, the country was on the verge of rockin' round the clock with Bill Haley and the Comets, and the personal computer had not yet been invented. It was a world waiting for the explosion of the electronic microchip age, and Buck Rodgers was to be one of the knights of its untarnished top brass.

"It was an exciting time," says Rodgers, "and I was one of the few marketing experts in 'stored program machines.'" Rodgers sold the smaller version of this engineering marvel for two years before getting his first big break. He captained the team that installed one of the first large-scale computers, an IBM 705, in a Westinghouse Electric plant in Sharon, Pennsylvania. It took up thousands of square feet and relied on vacuum-tube technology.

The year and a half it took for installation and the 90-day shakedown after it was in, plus the success of the whole operation, caught the eye of IBM's executive vice president, L. H. Lamotte. Rodgers soon became an administrative assistant to one of IBM's builders, and the rest, as they say, is history.

"From him, I learned to clearly articulate what it was I wanted people to accomplish," Rodgers says. Following in his mentor's path, Rodgers never set more than five goals at any one time, and he never delegated more than that magic number to any subordinate either. "You have to make the choice," explains Rodgers, "between desirability and necessity."

It was during an early stint as branch sales manager that Rodgers developed the belief that a company's organizational structure should be inverted, with the customer at the top and sales reps and management underneath. Rodgers' commitment to the customer even went as far as to give priority to appointments with customers when they conflicted with meetings in the IBM executive suite.

Rodgers once promised an aircraft manufacturer in Seattle that, if it would buy the IBM product, he would personally fly there every 30 days for six straight months to ensure the success of a complex computer installation. That condition helped make the sale, and Rodgers kept his word. He is a man given to keeping his word, showing up for meetings on time, and remembering appointments.

In this exclusive interview, Buck Rodgers talks about the past and the present, about what makes IBM one of the greatest institutions of our age, and the part that he has played in this long-running corporate hit.

Question: Since the year you began your career, tens of thousands of marketing people were hired by IBM in the United States. What do you think allowed you to go to the very top marketing position in the company?

Rodgers: There were two things—commitment and integrity. I never failed to meet objectives, I never failed to be on time for meetings. I tried to do the little things well, and the customers always knew they could count on me. So could the people I worked with at IBM. They didn't have to write me a lot of letters to get things done. The same is still true today. People who call me on the phone with a problem know it's going to be taken care of.

Question: When you were hired, was it your dream to one day be the top marketing person at IBM?
Rodgers: No, that came after I had been through several field assignments. I hoped someday to be president of IBM's computer operations. But I decided that the only way to achieve that was to do the best job in each position I held.

Question: That's a good attitude to have.
Rodgers: I have always had a positive attitude. I feel there isn't any problem that can't be solved with common sense and a little sweat.

Question: How do you develop this winning attitude?
Rodgers: A lot of it comes from inside the individual. But there are ways you can bring out a person's innate strengths. For myself, I have always had a talent for speaking. I never use any notes or a podium. I walk around. I've never had any special training. But public speaking is an ability that I have developed and made good use of.

Question: So developing a special talent in one area will help you in other areas?
Rodgers: Yes, always, but you need the desire to excel— at least to live up to one's own expectations. A lot of my success has been luck, and a lot of it turns out to be that I performed in an exemplary way in every job I was given. I wasn't afraid to fail.

Question: Did your parents instill a strong desire in you to be an achiever or a winner? To be somebody?

Rodgers: Yes, I think they did. All my life I played sports. I was all-state in football, captain of the basketball team, president of the class for four years. I played football in college, and today I run five miles, six times a week, and I'm an avid golfer and tennis player. I sort of compete with myself, but not to an obsessive point.

Question: It sounds like you derive a pleasure and satisfaction from being fully functioning!

Rodgers: I agree with that. I spend a lot of time on college campuses talking about changing values. I think people are trying to find the right balance in their lives. They expect to work for fair wages, but they don't want to sacrifice family life for their jobs. I also feel it's important to pay what I call "civic rent." To me, this is teaching young people. To others it may be involvement in programs dealing with drug abuse or mental health. Balance is important in life, and I think people at all ages are seeking that today.

Question: The IBM philosophy of business has become almost legendary. What makes it so special?

Rodgers: It is based on three beliefs; first, to respect the individual; second, to give the best service of any company in the world; and third, to expect excellence from what people do. This was the idea of Tom Watson, Sr., when he started the business back in 1914. He said that if you're going to do business with the IBM Corporation, you ought to feel that you're getting value and exceptional service. It is a desire to do things right the first time that permeates the business.

Question: What impressed you personally about IBM?

Rodgers: When I was being interviewed in college, I had never heard of IBM, and I decided to go with them because I was intrigued by their philosophy, and I was impressed with the quality of the IBM people that I met.

Question: Were there any myths about the company that you found were not true?

Rodgers: There is one [he chuckles] and that's the IBM dress code. They don't have any policy that says you've got to wear a white shirt or a dark suit or a sincere tie. IBM really doesn't care what people look like, and I don't either, as long as they dress with taste. You want the customer to concentrate on what you're saying, not on what you look like. Even so, up until the time I retired, I wore a lot more white shirts than I did blue!

Question: You said that your first position at IBM was as a "marketing representative." You didn't say "sales rep."

Rodgers: At IBM we called our people "marketing reps." There is a distinction between *marketing* and *selling*. *Selling*, to me, is the art of persuasion. That's the ability through personal attributes to convince someone that they need to buy the product or service that you're offering. *Marketing*, to me, is a more all-encompassing term. It means understanding the customers, speaking their language, putting together a cost-justified solution, and most of all being able to give value. IBM doesn't sell products. At IBM, people sell solutions to a set of problems. What the customer wants to know is how you can improve the inventory turnover rate, or lower costs—how you can help a business better serve its own customers.

Question: There are so many selling concepts in this country: nonmanipulative selling, the soft sell, consultative selling, situational selling, and so on. But you seem to be zeroing in on solution-oriented selling.

Rodgers: That's what IBM's training program is all about. You've got to speak the language that the customer understands. The days of Willy Loman are long gone— today you have to go in and think, "How can I, in some way, with my thinking and my products, give value and service to this particular customer?" Those who do that are the individuals who are going to succeed.

Question: What are your own personal principles of persuasion—ones that work well for you?

Rodgers: I try to be a reasonably good listener. I try to get the customer to have confidence in me as an individual. I try to convince people that I am interested in them and their problems. I share ideas and then try to get them to share theirs. Then I try to find answers to their problems. Too many times people don't get the chance to say what's on their minds. When the salesperson gives the customer the "fire hose approach," that's missing what might have been the real hot button you were looking for.

Question: Good listening establishes trust and confidence.

Rodgers: But it's the hardest thing in the world to do, especially for people who have a lot of ideas and are enthusiastic. It's very difficult for all of us.

Question: I understand that the training program for an IBM marketing rep takes one whole year. How is it structured?

Rodgers: The first 30-day period is an orientation into IBM's culture and history. After that, the new reps go off to Atlanta or Dallas for 30 days, where they start to learn about the products and selling techniques. Then they go back to the branch office, where they apply what they have learned in the classroom. They work with the marketing reps and systems engineers on real-life proposals, and they work with customers. After about three months, they go back to the classroom for another 30 days of application orientation, plus they find out what the competitive world is all about. During this time they are alternating between theory and practicality. IBM tries to get its marketing reps to understand the terms and conditions and the resources available to them. The entire process is very competitive, and they're on their feet as much as possible. When they're through, they are totally confident about the products and the competition, and, above all, they are application oriented.

Question: What you seem to be saying is that this kind of totally focused training translates into a professional solution-oriented attitude.

Rodgers: That's right. You don't go from one level to the next at IBM until you have been tested and proven ready to make that step. It's a positive type of reinforcement. I've seen very fine organizations give little attention to initial training, let alone continuing education. If there's no structure or discipline—it won't work. We found out there are two things in a business that you increase out of proportion to the growth rate of the company: one is education, the other is communication. You train people well and communicate your goals to them.

Question: What is the relationship between the trainer in the classroom and the line manager in the branch office?

Rodgers: The line manager has the responsibility to see that the individual completes the training and that he or she is self-sufficient. The people at the education centers are responsible for making sure that the student is getting the basic fundamentals.

Question: Who does the actual sales and marketing training at the centers?

Rodgers: IBM takes the best people from their sales force, people who have an ability to express themselves, and gives them training assignments from 18 to 24 months. They become role models who can convey actual field experience. Marketing training is very sought after at IBM because it's a stepping-stone to a line-management position or to moving up in the business.

Question: That's a very unusual concept.

Rodgers: Most companies are reluctant to take their top producers out of the field and put them in education assignments. IBM says you must do this. Whatever the short-term effect, it will pay back tenfold by having knowledgeable representatives interfacing with the customer.

Question: So your best marketing reps seek out the function of trainer to go higher up the ladder?

Rodgers: That's right. They don't get stale in the process, and you keep a small number of professional educators, and the rest are fresh, new, and enthusiastic.

Question: Any manager who has been out of selling for more than two or three years tends to get out of touch with the marketplace.

Rodgers: IBM has a management system in which the top officers—the president, the heads of engineering/ manufacturing divisions, the heads of finance, personnel— are assigned specific customers. They work with these customers, but always through the marketing rep in the branch office. This keeps top management from being in an ivory tower, out of touch with reality. The other bonus is that the branch manager can use that top executive to cut through the bureaucracy. If the branch manager needs something done, he or she can go directly to that individual. It sounds so simple, but, believe me, it's done in very few organizations.

Question: You coined a wonderful term and I'd like to ask you about it. You once said that people in companies sometimes suffered from "psychosclerosis."

Rodgers: Yes—that means a "hardening of the attitudes," when people begin to feel they no longer can affect what goes on in an organization, when bureaucracy takes over. That's why IBM pulls people out of their protected little corners. The secret is to move people back and forth between various functions and disciplines. This broadens the person and provides fresh insights.

Question: What are some of the incentives that IBM uses to inspire the people in sales and marketing?

Rodgers: First, people are paid well for what they do. IBM has a salary and incentive structure that is split approximately 50/50. It is a "pay-for-performance" philosophy—the more you install, the more you make. Also, IBM pays its people more than other comparable companies pay.

Question: And then what else do they offer?

Rodgers: The most important is a meaningful and challenging assignment; beyond that is one of the best benefits programs in any industry. However, there is something I call the "take back." Any time a piece of equipment is discontinued or cancelled, no matter how long it has been installed for, the marketing rep who is on that account is charged back with the original commission. This makes sure that when the reps take over an account, they provide outstanding service. Most of IBM's business is based on repeat orders so the customer is only going to buy as long as he is satisfied.

Question: That's a tough rule.

Rodgers: Yes, it is, but it worked for as long as I was with IBM.

Question: What are some of the other forms of incentive?

Rodgers: There's the 100 Percent Club. This is important because it's the way to be recognized by peers and eventually be promoted. IBM strives to have between 70 and 75 percent of their people make their objectives and attend the 100 Percent Club. They also have a Golden Circle. IBM takes the top 10 percent of its sales force from around the world, with their spouses, to a five-day recognition event in exciting resort locations. It serves to recognize superior performance, but it also has a marketing purpose. You hear a lot of spouses saying, "You better bring me back here next year."

Question: I understand that you have one other form of incentive that is very popular with the salespeople.

Rodgers: You must be talking about what I call the "Lightning Strikes" program. Managers at all levels are given a dollar budget to recognize people on the spot who have demonstrated extraordinary effort. It might be for a new account or for helping a customer with a special problem. The support people can get these awards too. It's a night on the town, dinner, a show. They can range from a simple thank you to several thousand dollars handed out for unusual acts of heroism.

Question: It sounds like IBM is run like a small company.
Rodgers: That's right. When IBM was small, top management ran the company as if it were big; now that IBM is big, management runs it as if it were small. For example, they never let a branch office get above a certain size. Also, every effort is made to maintain a manager-to-person ratio of about 1 to 120.

Question: What do you think salespeople should be taught about selling that they are generally not taught?
Rodgers: Two things come to mind. First, concentrate on what the product will do, not what it is. The customer is only interested in results. Second—develop a financial capability. Due to a wide variety of terms and conditions available today, a key part of the selling business is an ability to clearly portray the right method of financial acquisition.

Question: Can you talk a little bit about how you helped the IBM rep identify with the total marketing philosophy?
Rodgers: Again, the key is feedback. Every 90 days, IBM asks all of its marketing reps and systems engineers to review the organization from a customer-satisfaction

perspective. They are asked to tell what they think of management's capability, quality of products, and the responsiveness of the support structure. This input is then matched against a similar set of survey questions that have been responded to by customers. This gives top management a good idea of any negative trends. The main objective is to take preventive action and correct the problems, plus to focus on the strengths.

Question: What was the biggest disappointment you ever suffered in your career?

Rodgers: That's a tough question. At one point I was interested in running the IBM Corporation. That didn't happen, but it never really affected my style of management or the way I performed on a daily basis. If I ever got shot out of the saddle, and that happens to everybody, the secret was to be able to get right back on the horse. A lot of people don't do that, they get gun shy instead. They start to worry and play it safe. You have to expect disappointments and frustrations in your life.

Question: In some people it leads to depression, and in others it seems to lead to increased ambitions.

Rodgers: If you have the philosophy that you're going to enjoy life, and do the best you possibly can—it's going to pay off for you in the long run.

Question: What is the core of your belief system, if you had to sum it up in one basic principle?

Rodgers: The thing I stress all the time is that you have to do a thousand things 1 percent better, not just do one thing 1,000 percent better. It's doing the little things well, being on time for meetings, returning phone calls, saying "thank you" to people. It sounds like a simplistic cliché, but that is the reason one organization or one person is successful and another is not. The secret is that everybody knows what they ought to be doing, but the ones who practice daily excellence are the real "difference makers."

Question: It sounds like a game of inches—like a constant victory over yourself.

Rodgers: That's true. And that's why I find the line between success and failure, whether it's personal or business, so thin that you often don't know what side of the line you're on. With a little extra effort and a positive attitude, the problem goes away. But some people never seem to understand that point.

ACTION PLAN

- When you are having a difficult time solving a problem, focus on your attitude. Can you improve your attitude in order to come up with a solution?
- Look at ways you can develop a talent in one area; then, see how you can apply this talent to other areas.
- Every customer interaction is an opportunity for developing your listening skills. When working with customers, let them share their thoughts with you first before you speak.
- Practice the "Lightning Strikes" program. When people do extraordinary work, recognize them on the spot and reward them with a meaningful gift.

CHAPTER 9

TONY SCHWARTZ

*The master of persuasion, Tony Schwartz shows
how to make the "deep sell."*

IN THE FIELD OF PERSUASION Tony Schwartz occupies a unique position. He can sell soap and political candidates with equal ease, and when asked how he persuades so convincingly, he answers with a smile, "I don't use manipulation at all. I think it is better to get people to do things for their own reasons."

He has been responsible for some very revolutionary concepts in the field of persuasion. It is around the foundation that he and Marshall McLuhan created together that our media-oriented society now functions.

Ideas like the global village, communicating through media, and persuading by leaving things out rather than by densely packing information—these suggest only a smattering of the concepts that Tony Schwartz initiated. He differentiates between the *hard sell*, the *soft sell*, and—his sell—the *deep sell*. Schwartz uses his knowledge of how our minds function, along with his extraordinary facility with media, to sell deep into the "nonconscious" (Schwartz prefers this to "unconscious") mind.

Schwartz is not an easygoing person. One senses his intensity and questioning nature immediately. He has no interest in flattering or cajoling. It seems to make little difference to him whether he's easy or hard to work with. He doesn't measure success by the number of goods sold by any one of his ads. He is interested in people's motives. He looks for what makes them move. He investigates their underlying needs and desires. Then he goes to his laboratory, the sound studio, to develop new ways to reach them.

There's a lot to be learned from this man, but he does not offer a facile kind of quick mental fix. He is not interested in motivating us. He has made a significant contribution to contemporary society and can help us know more thoroughly who we are. He is therefore worth our attention. Schwartz is a media genius. Though you may not know his face, at some time one of his TV or radio ads has surely precipitated your decision to buy. Tony Schwartz is the man called in to make the media pitch for a range of products, from cold cream to Dream Whip, from Democrat to Republican. In some cases, his political ads have received so much attention that the opposing forces in the campaign have had to change strategy in midstream.

As Schwartz stated in an interview with the *Washington Post*, "I was the first one to do commercials for the American Cancer Society dealing with emotions rather than medical facts." He was likewise the first to use a real child's voice in a commercial rather than follow tradition and use a woman imitating a child. And he claims the educators are mistaken in fighting television; he believes they should be using it.

Schwartz has written eloquently about the media, post-literate society, TV, radio, commercials, and a host of other topics in his books, *Media*, *The Second God*, and *The Responsive Chord*. He has been interviewed and quoted widely, and he was the subject of an hour-long Bill Moyers' special on PBS.

Schwartz is a pioneer whom many consider a genius. Together with Marshall McLuhan, he developed many of the media techniques we take for granted today, and he continues in his quests for the new truths in media. He is a practical intellectual—a rare spirit who approaches his own sales record in an offhand way.

As Schwartz himself says, "I don't use manipulation. I use *partipulation*. I let people know about the things they need and they make their own decisions."

In this exclusive interview, Tony Schwartz, media mastermind, shares his unique approach to selling.

Question: How many radio and TV commercials have you created?

Schwartz: I would say over 20,000. I like to say that I've written more best sellers than anyone else in the world.

Question: One of the things you're so well known for is your ability to bring to the surface people's feelings, conflicts, and emotions through your radio commercials. How do you do that?

Schwartz: I have found that anything you can do with pictures you can also do with sound. Let's take a normal

Dream Whip commercial. The script reads, "Dream Whip—only 14 calories per tablespoon." Usually this line will be given a literal reading. But I ask, "What is the announcer really saying?" He's really saying. "You don't have to worry if you eat Dream Whip. You won't get fat." So, you want to use what I call an *environmental reading*—a reading that relates to the real world, the world we live in. You want to read it like a woman who's on a diet sharing the news with a fat friend. "Dream Whip has only 14 calories per tablespoon!" Or take Bufferin for another example. "Got a headache? Come to Bufferin." You need to read it like "Got a headache? Come to Mama." That's one level.

Question: Is that an unconscious level?

Schwartz: I don't like the word "unconscious." I prefer the word "nonconscious." For instance, if you asked me to name all the tapes in my office, I could tell you maybe 500 or 1,000. Then suppose you said, "But what about that one with the man from India?" I'd say, "Oh yes. I remember that one." I just wouldn't have been conscious of it.

Question: How do you evoke a feeling from the listener?

Schwartz: It has to do with the difference between *learned recall* and *evoked recall*. For example, when my mother went to a store with a shopping list, the storekeeper would take her order, then go back and get the stuff and come out. Radio and TV advertising eliminated the need for the salesclerk and made the stockroom into the store. When you walk through and see the various items, you can say, "Hey, we're out of cereal." Commercials evoke the connection of the product to your life, and once you're in the store, the products evoke both the commercial and your own experience.

Question: Can the same techniques you use in commercials be used in person-to-person selling?

Schwartz: They are all the time. People in all areas of life use them.

Question: In your book, **Media, The Second God,** *you wrote that you use customers as a work force. What do you mean by that?*

Schwartz: Here's an example. [*Plays a tape of a commercial.*] "You know, there are two men running for Congress in the 6th district. Bob Carr and Charles Chamberlain. Mr. Chamberlain has been in Congress for over 12 years. Let me read you a list of things he's accomplished. [*Dead silence on the tape for a few seconds.*] You see—that's exactly why this message is paid for by a growing number of Republicans and Democrats who want Robert Carr elected to Congress." Presearch* had showed that only 1 person in a 100 could remember one thing that Chamberlain had done in 12 years in Congress. So I used the audience as a work force. I let them participate in the commercial.

Question: How would you describe this process?

Schwartz: I'm allowing people's associations, or lack of associations, to surface. This enables them to use those associations as part of their thinking. Another factor that I find fantastic in communication is shame. It was the most effective means of social control in primitive cultures. I used it in many commercials.

---

*Editor's note: Presearch, briefly defined, is research conducted before the actual broadcast of a commercial.

Question: What would be an example of this?

Schwartz: Listen to this commercial. "Let me ask you something. Have you ever seen someone allow his dog to go on the sidewalk? Sometimes right in front of a doorway, maybe your doorway? Did it make you angry? Well, don't get angry at the poor soul. Feel sorry for him. He's just a person who's not able to train his dog. He's just not capable of it. In fact, after he's had his dog for a short time, what happens? The dog trains him. So the next time you see a person like that on the street, take a good look at him and while you're looking, feel sorry for him because you know he just can't help himself, even though he might like to. Some people are strong enough and smart enough to train their dogs to take a few steps off the sidewalk. Other people aren't. Makes you wonder, doesn't it, if the master is at the top of the leash or the bottom of leash." Most people would have said, "You shouldn't let your dog do this." But I said, "You shouldn't should on people." Then I thought, "What could I do to make this person not let his dog do this?" People don't like to be told that they should do something. You're much better off if you can cause them to do it for their own reasons.

Question: Isn't that a form of manipulation?

Schwartz: I don't think the word is accurate. *Partipulation* is the word I'd use to describe the process. A group of people once told me that they don't pay any attention to TV commercials. I asked them what kind of toothpaste they used. They all said Crest. At that time Crest was only being advertised on TV. Partipulating is when the listener becomes an active part of the selling process.

Question: You have studied sounds for many years. From the listener's point of view, when does sound become noise?

Schwartz: Long before the Electronic Age, when someone heard a drunk coming home singing, it used to be sound. When Barbra Streisand singing on the radio became more interesting, then the drunk became noise. Just interchange the word *noise* for the word *sound* and you find the real meanings. For instance, the noise of children—the sound of children. People often talk of the clutter factor on radio, but I have no problem with that. If I presearch people's interests, I know what will reach them. If I also do a media profile of the people I presearch, I know what stations they listen to, what magazines they read, and so on. I know what they will mentally tune in to and what they will tune out.

Question: Do you think that the media shape our expectations?

Schwartz: No. I don't. I think that it fulfills them. When kids watch TV, they get a good feeling when they see things they use. "We eat that cereal. Mom drives that car."

Question: Who created the "deep sell"?

Schwartz: I did. I say I'm not interested in hard or soft sell. I'm interested in deep sell. Sometimes deep may come from hard, sometimes from soft. For instance, people don't remember radio as a source of information the way they do newspaper or magazines. They may not consciously listen to radio. They bathe in it—are surrounded by it—in the same way that people at home may have the soap operas on TV while they do their chores. I call this a *surround*. People hear what relates to their experience and interest; therefore participation is deep into their mind. That's one example of deep sell.

Question: In an interview with Bill Moyers, you said that no one has experience with answers to problems. They have experience with only the problems. What did you mean by that?

Schwartz: We talked about creating commercials for politicians. Often people think that the politicians should use commercials to give answers to problems. First, the politicians don't have answers. Second, if they gave the answers, people couldn't identify with the commercials because they don't have experience with the answers—only with the problems. So the best commercial is one that makes people feel that the candidate is qualified, and once they feel he or she is capable and qualified, then you want them to feel that the candidate feels the same way they do about the problem.

Question: What does that do to the listener?

Schwartz: When the politician tells how he feels about the problem, the response is, "He feels the same way I do about that—he'll do the right thing."

Question: What are your ethical standards in creating a commercial?

Schwartz: I would never do anything to anyone else that I wouldn't like done to me. I wouldn't do certain ads. I wouldn't do cigarette ads or any ads for a candidate who was opposed to a mutually verifiable nuclear freeze.

Question: What's your measure of success?

Schwartz: Personally, I think being able to earn a living and bring up my family and buy the things that they need.

To be a good neighbor and a good person. I do as much free work as I do paid work.

Question: What's your professional measure of success?

Schwartz: I'm very interested in using media for social change. I did a campaign in Massachusetts two years ago to help the state government make up for what Reagan cut out of the budget for aid to education for students. I got $34 million two years ago for student aid for education. Last year I did it again and got $50 million for the same thing. I do work for the hospitals here in New York City, for the fire department and for the police.

Question: Do you derive meaning from positive social change?

Schwartz: Yes. The school across the street was voted out of existence. I thought it was an important school—it was training the police and firefighters. So I did a campaign, and we saved the school.

Question: In your book you quoted Daniel Boorstin, "Technology is a way of multiplying the unnecessary." Then you added, "Technology in advertising creates progress by developing the need for the unnecessary." Do you feel you dedicate your life to creating needs for the unnecessary?

Schwartz: No, I'm not doing that. Maybe some people are selling products that people don't need. I attach to real things in people. I do best with products where I can let people know about the things they need. I tell them about what products can do and then they make their own decisions.

ACTION PLAN

- When making a sale, look deep to discover the true concerns of your customer. Address those concerns with the language you use.
- Look for ways to make the deep sell: Find ways to make your products or services more meaningful to the customer's "nonconscious" mind.
- Strive for the highest ethical standards. Never do anything that you wouldn't want done to you or that infringes on the rights of others or that violates the law. Learn your company's ethical guidelines and follow them.

CHAPTER 10

LONNIE "BO" PILGRIM

*The key to sales success is to use integrity
in every situation.*

WHEN LONNIE "BO" PILGRIM was barely nine years of age, his father suddenly died, leaving Lonnie's mother and her seven children to struggle for themselves. "I had to grow up quickly," he said with a distant look as he contemplated his past. Pilgrim's humble beginnings, and his faith in a higher power that helps us use our innate gifts, have enabled him to build an empire that is rock solid.

A practical man, Pilgrim has combined a savvy sense of what the market wants with the creativity to expand his product base by stretching the limits of what can be done with ordinary chicken. In the otherwise pedestrian field of chicken production and distribution, he is a unique figure. Doing a million dollars of business a day is no mean feat.

Pilgrim thrives on such superlative performance. His boneless chicken—that's right, whole chicken sold with the skin on and no bones at all—has broken sales records in the Texas stores that are lucky enough to stock it.

How did he create such a rare bird? By trying thousands of different ways to bone a chicken, by leaving the skin intact, and by doing it in as little time as possible for peak efficiency. Pilgrim took home two chickens a night for months, practiced deboning them in his kitchen, invented special tools for the job, and finally got it down to a science. He then taught his factory workers how to duplicate the performance, and, presto, a new product, which created new and expanded markets, was born.

Pilgrim's successful venture into the previously untapped market of Mexico to sell eggs would never have come to pass if he hadn't had the courage to try. He might never have tried if he hadn't taken other risks and been successful before. Bo Pilgrim has tried and failed many times. He knows that failure need not be devastating. He has experienced its bite, and he knows that wounds can be healed by trying again and getting it right.

As he puts it, "We would not be at the top of our industry without our high standards for efficiency. We salvage everything but the squawk." Bo Pilgrim, who started selling before age nine, has turned a small feed store into a major company with an astonishing $1 million a day sales volume from the sale of chicken (½ million per day) and table eggs (100,000 dozen per day).

Many of Bo Pilgrim's 2,500 employees have surpassed his high school education with grades, diplomas, and degrees; yet he leads his entire conglomerate based on the simple lessons he has learned in years of self-education and a few specialized seminars. His company's slogan, "Honest Chicken from Real Pilgrims," reflects the deeply ingrained values inherited from his father, who earned the admiration and respect of his community through his high standards of integrity. It is no wonder that Pilgrim Industries has made "integrity" a major pillar of its official marketing philosophy. The company brochure proudly dictates: "Our whole philosophy at Pilgrim is based on never promising more than we can deliver. And delivering everything that we promise. Living up to our commitments—honestly. That's the way we operate."

There is much to learn from the way Bo Pilgrim operates. He doesn't mince words. This interview provides a rare opportunity to trace the successful steps of a sales superstar.

Question: Your company specializes in selling chicken and eggs. What is your current sales volume?

Pilgrim: We are producing a half a million chickens a day and 100,000 dozen table eggs. Our volume is about $1 million in sales a day.

Question: Do you remember your first sale ever?

Pilgrim: My father was postmaster, and he ran a general merchandise store in a little community. He would tell me that I could earn one soft drink for every five drinks I sold. So I made myself a little cart and went three-fourths of a mile down the road to the cotton gin, which was run by my grandfather. I spent about 30 minutes and sold five drinks for a nickel each. When I got back to the store, I would give my daddy the money, and he'd give me my drink. That turned me on to selling. One of my first sales goals in life was to earn enough money to be able to walk up to the drink box and buy a cola any time I wanted to without having to ask my daddy.

Question: When did you reach your first sales goal?
Pilgrim: Within a couple of years. Before my father died, I was working for him in the summertime hanging potato sacks on a grader. I earned $1 a week, and at the end of the week, I could go to town with someone and buy a chicken fried steak for 35 cents with all the trimmings and spend 15 cents for the show.

Question: How old were you when your father died?
Pilgrim: I was nine years old when he died on April 11, 1939. There were seven kids in the family, the youngest only six months old. Only one was already married, so things were a little rough. My mother had only $80 in savings. I had to work my way through high school. It was a matter of survival. My mother remarried, but I didn't accept the marriage, so I left home to live with my grandmother.

Question: What did your grandmother do?
Pilgrim: She was a housewife. I remember her dealing with a peddler who visited us with his truck. We raised chickens in the backyard, and the peddler would buy them or trade for supplies. He went down the road and sold the chickens to someone else. This created some interest for me.

Question: When did you start your own business?
Pilgrim: My brother and I bought an old feed store back in the mid-1940s. We started out selling horse feed, dairy

feed, and chicken feed. In 1950, we built our own feed mill to expand our business. In 1951, I went into the Army and spent two years in California. I noticed that they used a better system for feeding chickens. Back home, we were handling feed in 100-pound bags, by hand; out there, they were conveying feed automatically from a feed tank. When I came home in 1953, I installed a feed tank and tied it in with an automatic feeder regulated by a time clock. We were selling a lot of people on using this new system because they didn't have to be there to feed the chickens.

Question: *What kinds of goals did you set for your business during this phase?*

Pilgrim: I wanted to do more volume, I wanted to give my customers more value than they could get from our competition, I wanted to give them good, personal service, and at the same time I wanted to make a profit. But the most important item on my list was integrity.

Question: *Why?*

Pilgrim: My father taught me that by his actions. For 10 years after he died, everyone was telling me about his high standards for integrity. Moral values became real important to me early. The disappointment of my father's dying led me to join the church, and I said to myself and God that if I ever achieved anything, I'd certainly want to recognize Him as being a partner with me in that journey. He didn't go out and part any waters for me, but I've always had this concept that He knows what's going on and He gives us a brain to decide. We have to make decisions and choices throughout our lives.

Question: And you became a decision maker at a very early age.

Pilgrim: I have always taken a position of leadership. When I was a kid, I would always hold up my hand and ask the others to team up with me as the leader of the group. It didn't make any difference whether we were playing a game or not. It was instinct.

Question: I can see that you have a lot of drive and ambition.

Pilgrim: I always had a lot of drive. I remember when I came back from the Army, my brother told me that he'd like to sell out to me. I asked him why. He said, "Bo, you have so much ambition to be rich, it just drives me up the wall." Luckily, I talked him out of it, and I told him that I needed him as my senior partner.

Question: Did other people think the same way about you?

Pilgrim: A friend of mine once told me that some day I'd be worth a million dollars because of my drive.

Question: You said earlier that your first financial goal was to be able to buy your own cola. What was your second goal?

Pilgrim: My second goal was to make a million dollars.

Question: When did you reach it?

Pilgrim: In the early 1960s. After I made my first million dollars, I said, "Maybe I can make $10 million." After I made $10 million, my next goal was to make $10 million a month. I'm proud to say that I've reached all these goals.

Question: We talked about your automatic feed system and how it increased sales. What was your next growth step?

Pilgrim: In the 1950s we started to own the chickens and put them out to the growers. We'd furnish the feed and pay them so much per pound for growing the chickens.

Question: How about your competition?
Pilgrim: When we started out in this area, there were about 20 other companies in the chicken-and-egg business, among them very big firms like Quaker and Ralston-Purina. Now, we're the only ones left who produce chickens in northeast Texas.

Question: How did you outsell your competitors?
Pilgrim: I viewed my competitors as a challenge—I didn't expect them to go away. I had to look for new ideas to beat them in quality, service, and price. I used to say about the quality of our feed, "I won't ship a sack of feed that I can't taste myself." If I lost a customer to Purina, I tried to figure out some way to get that customer back. I worked hard at coming up with better ways to serve each customer's needs. I think the main reason my competitors disappeared is because we were willing to give more for the dollar.

Question: How have you been able to build a successful business on such a limited product line?
Pilgrim: There are two things. First, selling. Selling creates a new frontier, it creates new life. Second, we've built our business on the cost side. We've out-produced others based on cost. My philosophy has been that you'll survive in this industry only if you can maintain your cost level within the top third of the industry. You can't be average in

selling and average in cost if you want to survive. I've always preached to my people that we're not performing until we get into the top third.

Question: How do you reach the top third?

Pilgrim: The key lies in having a management control system and having managers who understand those goals and perform in that direction. I attended many American Management Association seminars and designed our own MBO (management by objectives) system. I also set up a monthly award system where we compare actual performance versus goals. If my managers meet the goals, they'll receive a bonus check at the end of the month.

Question: What other factors have contributed to your reaching the top?

Pilgrim: We diversified. We began to own our distribution network. We built our own rendering plant, we began to control the breeder farms, then we raised laying hens and sold table eggs. My goal was to have an integrated operation, I always wanted to do the whole thing—play every golf ball on the course. We went into the trucking business, since we thought that we could operate our own trucks more efficiently. We bought a Chevrolet dealership, and in 1969 I bought a bank to handle some of our money needs. I always thought that I could do for myself just as well and as economically as someone else on the outside could do for me.

Question: Do you consider yourself a good salesperson?

Pilgrim: I guess it's just been second nature to me. You have to be able to sell your ideas to reach the top.

Question: What are the qualities of a good salesperson?

Pilgrim: First, you have to understand people and their personalities. Second, you ought to understand what they need to buy, rather than what you want them to have. Third, you need to project to them that you can win their respect if given an opportunity. Don't ask for things up front, but ask for an opportunity.

Question: What was your biggest sale ever?

Pilgrim: In 1981, I went to Mexico to look at chicken operations and talked to various government officials about their needs for table eggs. I left with an order for 750 truckloads of eggs to be delivered to Mexico City in 90 days. No one had ever attempted to deliver $12 million worth of eggs to Mexico City before. I sold these eggs on an open account, and we did everything we told them we would do plus extra. They paid promptly, and we made an additional sale the following year. I treated them just like customers in Dallas or Los Angeles.

Question: What's your measure of success?

Pilgrim: My measure of success is based upon the results I can produce. Results are the product of ability plus experience times motivation. It's not necessarily measured in dollars.

Question: Why not?

Pilgrim: Money was never my No. 1 priority. I always looked at that as a by-product. I think someone who is driven by money becomes like H. L. Hunt, who brings his lunch in a brown sack. I always told myself, "I don't eat lunch out of a brown sack—I'd rather eat lunch at the Country Club." If money is going to be your driving force, you are going to become very conservative and try to hoard money. To me, money is something you use to make things happen. You can use it to build a business, to help others, or to give it to the preacher. I am not interested in storing money.

Question: You are currently introducing a very innovative and almost revolutionary product, the boneless chicken. How did you come up with this idea?

Pilgrim: About three years ago, we had a slowdown in sales, and I tried to find new ways to increase demand. I looked at how other countries sold chicken and found that 65 percent of all chickens sold in Japan were sold boneless. I searched for instructions to learn how to debone a chicken without cutting the skin or cutting the chicken in half. I started calling experts from all over the country and began to examine the existing methods for deboning chickens. Every evening, I took two chickens home with me to practice deboning until I could do it in less than 20 minutes. With help from people in our plant, we created special workbenches and tools to speed up the process even more. We can now debone a chicken without cutting the skin and leaving all the meat in its original position, in about 6 minutes. We named it "Bo Pilgrim's Boneless Miracle." We have applied for a patent for this new deboning process.

Question: How many people do you employ?
Pilgrim: About 2,500.

Question: Would you agree that a company is not as much influenced by the management in place as by the personality of its leader?

Pilgrim: I think that the personality of the chief executive certainly sets the tone for what is expected of employees.

Question: What is it that you expect of yourself?

Pilgrim: Business is like a game to me. I have a friend who plays golf every day. He is constantly trying to improve his score—so am I. Business is an extremely competitive game, and you can't daydream or assume that something is going to happen—you have to make it happen. If you lose, you just start preparing for the next game. Don't worry about the game you lost; it's the next one coming up that you prepare for. You have to stay in the top third to be recognized and to survive.

Question: So it appears that success begins by having high expectations of yourself.

Pilgrim: Yes. I had a guy once who quit on me and I asked him why. He said that I expected so much. I talked to him only once a week, but he perceived my expectations.

Question: How do you deal with adversity?

Pilgrim: I just accept it as a fact of life. It's inevitable. You can't change adversity. I devote my time and interest to those things that I can change.

Question: You are a positive thinker.

Pilgrim: Of course. I think it goes back to my childhood, when my father died ... it was a matter of survival.

Question: When you were nine years old, did you have a vision of what you were going to do today?

Pilgrim: I had a vision of being successful; however, not to this extent. I guess you could say that I have exceeded my dreams by far.

Question: What would you do differently if you had to start all over again?

Pilgrim: Obviously, education is more important today than when I started. I was an entrepreneur before I got out of high school. I would get a college education now if I had to do it over again.

Question: It sounds like you learned more out of necessity. What would you consider the key lessons that you've learned?

Pilgrim: First, you have to develop a high level of discipline and apply it to your personal, spiritual, and professional life. Just as the Bible has the Ten Commandments to follow, there are certain principles that apply to any business, like planning, organizing, motivating, problem solving, appraising performance, and so on. You can't just understand these principles from a textbook point of view. You have to go a step further and apply them consistently. There are many people who learn the basic principles and recite them, but they don't practice them.

Question: How do you go about translating this knowledge into action skills?

Pilgrim: We have developed an ongoing, everyday system and people can see it and become part of it. We select our people very carefully. We don't take long shots; we train them thoroughly; we give them an extensive orientation so each one understands the purpose of his or her job, responsibility, and authority. We agree on goals, and we measure them. So there is no one in our organization running around wondering what he or she is supposed to be doing.

Question: And you set the example.

Pilgrim: Yes. I don't ever ask a person to do anything that I am not willing to do myself. I think you can have all the company goals you want, but if a person doesn't get job satisfaction, you can forget it. You need to achieve job satisfaction and personal satisfaction or you're not motivated.

Question: What do you feel are the key motivating factors for your sales force?

Pilgrim: The two motivators in achieving our sales goals are monetary rewards and personal pride. I am proud of their ability to achieve results, they participate in the goal-setting process, and they are well rewarded for their achievements.

Question: How many hours do you work a day?

Pilgrim: I get up at 5:30 A.M. and I go to bed at 10 P.M. Most of the time, I am doing something that contributes to the business. I don't believe a successful business can be managed on 40 hours a week. If a manager is not working 60 hours a week, he's not doing his job. I tease my senior VPs with the saying, "Anything after 20 hours a day is free time."

Question: You're married and you've raised three children.

Pilgrim: We've been married nearly 30 years, and we have had less than six heated arguments and no walkouts.

Question: When you look at your family and compare raising three children with raising a company employing 2,500 people and reaching sales of $1 million a day, which do you consider the greater success?

Pilgrim: I wouldn't consider myself successful if I had gained the whole world and failed my family.

Question: How would you like to be remembered?

Pilgrim: I'd like to be remembered as a good father, as a religious person, and as an outstanding businessman of integrity.

ACTION PLAN

- Make a list of your own sales goals. Be sure to write down the date you've designated to achieve each goal. Also, differentiate among professional, financial, and personal goals.
- Write down ways that your competitors are currently meeting your customers' needs. Then write down how you can better meet those customer needs. Create action steps to implement your best ideas.
- Set up monthly award programs that compare actual performance versus goals.
- Measure success based on the results you can produce.
- Treat business like a competitive game: You have to make things happen. But if you lose, don't worry but instead prepare for the next game.
- Devote your time to what you can actually change.

CHAPTER 11

MO SIEGEL

The founder of Celestial Seasonings on overcoming
hardship by always striving to be the best.

M O SIEGEL is an enthusiastic purveyor of healthy products. One senses his excitement by the way he sips tea (as if he were tasting fine wine), by the rise in his voice when he describes the challenges of his business, and by his entire company's dedication to providing the best possible product and service for the consumer. But Mo is more than a one-dimensional picture of a business tycoon out to make a buck. Mo Siegel respects sound business principles and wants to make a profit, but he also wants to make a worthwhile contribution to the society that supports his work.

Perhaps it is this very combination that helped Siegel to weather the early struggles. At one point a single crop failure almost ruined his business. But, he didn't let that setback deter him from his ultimate goals, and he looks back to that time with a kind of reverence. In Mo's mind, the greatest affliction in life is never to have been afflicted. Said another way, we need afflictions to test and challenge us. Without them, we would have no measure of our own abilities—of our own creativity.

Siegel is an avid skier and cyclist, riding his bike to work and back home every day. He believes that wealth means little without health and that when an organization can attach itself to something greater than itself—to an overall concept of doing good for others—we will all profit.

This is a true rags-to-riches story about a boy with a dream, the man he became, and the success he built. With only a high school education and a dream to make his first million dollars by his 25th birthday, Mo Siegel started Celestial Seasonings in 1971. He was 20 then. He did it all on his own—took the risk, borrowed the money, developed the concept, and worked very hard until it became the reality he always knew it would. Mo Siegel's super success is a shining example of the opportunity that is open to anyone who looks for it.

This exclusive interview describes how he achieved his success without giving up his unique values and principles.

Question: You made your first million dollars at age 26. How do you explain that?

Siegel: I had an objective since about the age of 6 that by the age of 25, I would have made my first million. I think it was the first week after I turned 26 that I reached it on paper.

Question: How old were you when you started Celestial Seasonings?

Siegel: I was 20.

Question: When you started, what kind of goals or dreams did you pursue?

Siegel: From the very beginning, I would tell bankers, "I am out to build a $100 million company, and I am going to start with selling herb tea." They thought I had lost my mind.

Question: What made you decide to enter the herb tea business?

Siegel: Part of me wanted to go into an art-oriented field like the movies or greeting cards, and another part of me was very health driven. I knew as a child that I was going to be in business, and I've always had an inclination from a very young age for being philosophical. I finally decided that I could be much more useful as a person by being dedicated to health.

Question: It seems as though you had a good understanding of that market.

Siegel: I think I am fairly strategic when I look at a business. I saw the health opportunity very early. I looked at the European tea market and noticed that herb teas sold well, but Americans hadn't started to use them yet. I saw that more and more people were getting interested in health. They began to exercise, they took vitamins, and they became more health conscious.

Question: When you started Celestial Seasonings back in 1971, how did the people feel about herb teas?

Siegel: When I started, people still thought that herb teas were weird. In the consumer's mind, herb tea didn't taste very good, and you only drank it when you were sick. I wanted to make herb tea that tasted good and sell people on drinking it all the time.

Question: You must have faced a number of challenges.

Siegel: I remember when I went with my gunnysack collecting herbs in the mountains, many thought of me as an odd guy. But that's the price you pay when you introduce a new idea. Dr. Ken Cooper, the father of aerobics, told me once that when he went to Dallas to promote his fitness program, they thought he had lost his marbles. When I was out picking tea, I was the butt of countless Euell Gibbons jokes.

Question: They thought you were a health nut?

Siegel: No, I was a fanatic then; I am a health nut now.

Question: You have mellowed.

Siegel: Yes. In fact, I jokingly say these days that the reason I exercise, take my vitamins, eat my alfalfa sprouts, and drink my herb tea is for one simple reason: to be able to eat as much ice cream as I want.

Question: How did you sell your herb teas back when you started?

Siegel: I made cold calls on health food stores in my old Datsun. I love selling. I feel that I am doing something good for other people just by selling our product.

Question: But you are not only motivated by being good to other people?

Siegel: There is a battle that I go through sometimes. There is a part of me that clearly wants to make money, big money, and fairly fast. This part of me is motivated by achievement and ambition. The other part is altruistic—the need to do good.

Question: What would you consider to be the best approach in selling?

Siegel: I think it's not hard to sell if you are benefit oriented. I believe that nobody buys anything if there is not a benefit. I always say to our people, "If you can't give your customer a WIFM—the what's in it for me—don't show up." To make your sales calls meaningful, there should be a specific reason for the call besides the WIFM. Like something new, something different. I also have a rule in selling, that you should always make a friend.

Question: Build relationships.

Siegel: Yes. Make a friend, because if you don't get the sale, at least you've got a friend. Be close to your customers, care about them, service their needs.

Question: To what do you attribute your success?

Siegel: I think that either you follow the basic principles or you get nailed. There are some rules that work almost all the time. If you don't set goals, you don't get anywhere. That's so basic. The thing that I enjoy in my business is figuring out the overall mission, then establishing goals and developing the strategies, the action plans, and the calendar by which they must be completed. Another basic principle would be to be persistent in your work. To work smarter. Follow your priorities. Do No. 1, 2, and 3 first in the day. I go as far as putting time percentages next to the tasks. For example, I may decide to invest 40 percent of the working day in priority No. 1. At the end of the day I score how I've done for the day.

Question: So you know how well you've performed.

Siegel: I do the same with our business. I use the computer to measure our performance and compare it to that of other businesses. We are members of the Strategic

Planning Institute. According to their data, we rank in the upper 98 percent for productivity of all 2,000 companies that have been plugged into that model.

Question: What was your first major obstacle after you got your business started? Your first doubt that you'd ever reach your goals?

Siegel: I never thought that. Never. But we sure had a lot of obstacles,...although I finally concluded that the greatest affliction in life is never to have been afflicted. I give talks every so often on what I call the "10 principles of success." One of them is the acceptance of failure and persistence toward success. If you use a clear set of goals, you will reach about 85 percent of them, and 15 percent will be disappointments.

Question: How about your first major disappointment?

Siegel: Well, we once contracted a peppermint crop in Wisconsin because we were dissatisfied with our European imports. We bought the field standing, and then it rained for two weeks in August. Then a frost hit and we lost most of the crop. We almost went broke. That was our first major business failure. Nobody enjoys failing, but we can learn from what we do wrong, and in the process we find out how to get better.

Question: You use lemons to make lemonade.

Siegel: There are a lot of people who don't understand this principle. When they fail, they give up and seek shelter. For example, we worked over two years on developing a chamomile shampoo. We went through seven chemists to get the product that we wanted. We could have given up, but we persisted and asked: "What did we learn from the last failure? How can we do better?"

Question: What quality standards were you trying to reach?

Siegel: Very simple. We said that we wouldn't market our new product unless we could beat our competition in a blind test.

Question: How do you react when a competitor introduces a new line of herb teas? I see you as fairly competitive....

Siegel: I can't stand it, and I won't stop improving ours until we beat them. You're right—I am competitive. But I am only concerned with two areas: customer and product. I ask, "Is the customer happy?" and, "Are we making the best product?" That's all I care about.

Question: So instead of attacking the competition, you focus your energies on serving your customers better.

Siegel: Absolutely.

Question: What is it that you like most about your business?

Siegel: I want to establish a value system in our organization so that if I got hit on my bike someday, the value system would stay and the company would do well based on these values.

Question: What components would you include in this system?

Siegel: We've already developed a very detailed belief statement. You could compare it to four legs on a stool. The first leg is our love of our product. We are a product-driven company—we want to develop the best products. We are improving three of our four top sellers this year. Improving— and they weren't bad. People around here often ask, "If it isn't broken—why fix it?" To me, it doesn't count how good our products are; what counts is how good they can be. We constantly test our teas with thousands of people a year. We will not let anyone make a better cup of tea.

Question: What's your second leg?

Siegel: Our love of our customers and consumers. Our customers are the distributors. The consumer is the end user. We feel that if we can't sell benefits to the consumer, we shouldn't be in the business. We love to fill consumers' needs and benefit people. We are getting over 200 letters from consumers per week telling us that we're on the right track.

Question: If you don't serve a need, you won't be needed.

Siegel: If you're not filling needs, then you're tricking people. I'd rather die broke and be useful than make all the money in the world selling useless things. Our third leg is love of art and beauty. For example, we've developed this new package for restaurants, and it's probably the most beautiful tea package anybody has ever done. Four-color artwork on each packet. We use some of the best artists in the world for our packaging. The fourth leg is based on the dignity of the individual. If you develop work systems that dignify work and dignify individuals, life will certainly become more pleasant and also more productive. I guess some of my biggest disappointments have been in this area during my years as an entrepreneur. I've learned since that, as a manager, you should rise on people's shoulders, not around their necks.

Question: You don't have a business school education.

Siegel: No, I have only a high school education, but I think that if you want to have a good life, you have to learn from birth to the grave. One of my 10 rules of success is that you've got to learn and grow. I won't ride my bike to work without listening to educational tapes. I read all the time, I take classes, I just got into the Young President's Organization.

Question: What tapes do you listen to?
    Siegel: I love Dr. Norman Vincent Peale. I have over 30 of his tapes. I enjoy Peter Drucker.

Question: The best education is an open mind.
    Siegel: Yes, and to be able to use other people's minds. I have many heroes who have inspired me to grow in my business. For example, next week I will send out postcards to some 1,500 customers thanking them for their efforts. I hope by this summer I will have 10,000 customers on my postcard mailing list. I thought of it after I read Joe Girard and Mary Kay.

Question: Your employees receive a great deal of training.
    Siegel: Yes, I want my managers to have at least 30 hours of training per year. Salespeople should probably have more. I keep suggesting that they all have CD players in their cars, so that when they are stuck in traffic, they are getting smart.

Question: You developed a comprehensive value system for your company. How about your values as a person?
    Siegel: I think the greatest danger a person can have in his or her life is to become "I-important." The greatest satisfaction a person can have is to become selfless. The people who give are the happiest people in the world, not the people who take.

Question: How would money fit into this philosophy?

Siegel: I had this thought about my own values, and I pictured that I had died and gone to heaven. The ancients of days pulled out the record books, and they asked what I had done with my life. I said that I made a lot of money. They thumbed through the books, and said that they didn't see that. I said that I had sold more herb teas than anybody else, but they couldn't see that either. Then I said that I had dedicated my life to making people healthy, I had dedicated my life to being a true friend to people, a giving person, I had dedicated my life to my family, and they said that they saw that. When I went through this experience, I realized that you should check your values very carefully and do what is worthwhile to the world and not just worthwhile to you. A selfish life is a life not worth having.

Question: Meaning comes before money.

Siegel: I think so.

Question: What's your definition of success?

Siegel: As a corporation, measure it in sales, profits, and dignity of the individual. As a person, of all the greatest human achievements, the raising of a good family is the greatest achievement. You could build any size corporation imaginable and it would not equal the success of raising good children. That's the highest task a person could do in life.

Question: You have been raised by an older sister?

Siegel: Yes, my mother died when I was two years old.

Question: How large was your family?

Siegel: Four kids; two older sisters and one younger sister.

Question: What did your father do?

Siegel: He owned a kind of discount department store. He was an auctioneer. He did pretty well. He was a real driver. He worked like crazy all the time. He always thought that I was lazy. I do like to say that I never got one penny from him to build Celestial Seasonings.

Question: You had a tough childhood.

Siegel: I think I did. My father was such a driver. He was very hard for me to get along with. He had his set of views of the world. Anything that was different from those was not tolerated. From the age of 17, there was no further financial aid or anything else because my father and I had diametrically opposed views of religion. I ended up having a deep Christian faith while he's Jewish.

Question: You dealt with a number of big disappointments and had to grow up very fast.

Siegel: Yes. I have a painting of Abraham Lincoln in my office. He probably had about as many disappointments as anybody. But I believe that the disappointments hardest to bear are those that never come. It's never as bad as you anticipate it to be. I have always believed that you have to accept disappointments and failures in life. It's just part of the formula if you want to succeed. You've got to understand it and work with it.

Question: How did you learn to accept disappointments?

Siegel: I am basically religious. My views are very similar to Dr. Peale's. The foundation of his faith is not in materialism, it's not faith in people, but faith in God. I believe that people become greater by being more God-like rather than by becoming themselves. I don't believe that the self is everything or that by fulfilling yourself, you can be this great individual.

Question: How would you apply this faith to the reality of business?

Siegel: Well, take IBM as an example. Thomas Watson, Sr., said, "We will serve our customers better than any other corporation in the world." He made a philosophical statement that rallied the troops. He didn't say we are going to do really well and get rich. Or, it's going to be fun and you are all going to drive great cars. The point is, when an organization of people can attach themselves to something greater than themselves, the greater good comes of it. They perform much better, they go the extra mile because it's more fulfilling, and they are happier.

Question: It sets up a new perspective. You won't grow taller if you become the measure of all things. Are you saying that Abraham Maslow's theory of self-actualization is not necessarily motivating?

Siegel: I do like Maslow. What we need to learn is to balance ego-driven motivation and service motivation. When Watson said that he wanted to service his customers better, he revealed a lot of human ambition. He was able to reconcile his strong ambition to succeed with the desire to do something useful and valuable for other people. My goal is to achieve a balance between the two conflicting forces—a balance in which the giving is the greater force.

ACTION PLAN

- Look at the challenges you faced in your past. How did going through them make you stronger?
- Be motivated by being good to others.
- Make sales calls meaningful by showing customers their WIFM—what's in it for me.
- When you are selling, always make a friend.
- Set priorities at the beginning of the day. One, two, then three. At the end of the day, look back and score how you were able to stay on task.
- Always ask these two key questions: "Is the customer happy?" and "Are we making the best product or providing the best service?"
- Send postcards to your customers to thank them for their business.

CHAPTER 12

BARBARA PROCTOR

Sales advice on taking risks from the founder
of the first advertising agency run by an
African American woman.

B ARBARA PROCTOR is a demanding woman who has
little time for self-indulgence and less for self-pity. She
has spent a lifetime working her way up, and, by her own
admission, everything has been a piece of cake since she got
an education. Proctor started life in the most inauspicious
of circumstances. Dirt poor, black in the still-segregated
South, she was born to an unwed teenage mother, and yet
she rose to be the first African American woman to start her
own advertising agency. Her story is now well known, and
she tells it frequently, more to provide a positive role model
for other women than for any other motive.

Proctor is a woman who knows how to talk to anyone,
and she proved that when she had to go out to sell herself
as the owner of her own advertising agency. To say that it

was an uphill sell would be the greatest of understatements. She knew she could do a good job for her clients. She carried herself with pride and confidence, knowing these attitudes would be felt by others and would eventually land her the business she knew was out there.

The most important lesson to learn from Barbara Proctor's career can be summed up in one short piece of advice from her: "Take a risk." Women especially, according to Proctor, fear risk. They want guarantees, she says. But it has been a positive attitude toward taking risks that has allowed Barbara Proctor to succeed and flourish.

The determination to succeed creates that energy. It frees the mind and the soul. It lets us see clearly all the nuances of choice. Proctor walks with a firm step on ground made solid by enterprising and intelligent assessments of her own potential for growth and her own knowledge of what she has to offer. She knows there is much to be done and there are many ways to have an impact on her society. For her, nothing short of the very best will do. That will make life a little better for us all.

It was Barbara's grandmother who had the most lasting influence on her life. "She taught me that what is important is not on the outside, but inside. She said it is important to put something inside you, some courage, knowledge, or a skill—things that no one can take away," says the chief executive of Proctor & Gardner Advertising. Her grandmother used to say of her, "She ain't cute, but she's right smart, and one day she's going to amount to something."

Proctor left the mountains of North Carolina to attend Talladega College in Alabama. She intended to become a teacher. After finishing her undergraduate work in a brief three years, she added another year of psychology and sociology. A summer job at a camp in Michigan earned her enough money to get to Chicago, where she spent every penny. Although she intended to earn just enough to return to Black Mountain, North Carolina, instead, Barbara took a job writing the copy for record album covers. She's been a resident of the Windy City ever since.

Proctor's rise in the business world was steady. She grew like an oak tree planted in the sun. She spread her branches with each new spring. And she weathered many storms and cold winter nights. She met the kind of discrimination that black people have faced for centuries, and she met a new form of arrogance. Of this experience she says, "In advertising, the only thing worse than being a woman, was being an old woman. I was over 30, female, and black. I had so many things wrong with me that it would have taken all day to figure out which one to blame for my rejections. So I decided not to spend any time worrying about it."

She started her own advertising agency on $80,000 borrowed from the Small Business Administration. To secure the loan because she had no collateral, she went to three ad agencies and got job offers of $65,000, $80,000, and $110,000. She used the second as collateral—what she herself was worth on the open market.

The first account was hard to land. It took six months and much selling. "In every case where something would have been an obstacle, I've found a way to turn it to an advantage," says Proctor. "I say, if you decide you're a winner, then you are. If you decide you're a loser, you're right. I cannot buy the concept that anyone outside is responsible," she explains. Now, more than a decade later, her successful company is worth over $8 million and employs nearly 30 people.

Ethics plays an important role in Proctor's business life. "Advertising is the highest form of persuasion," she claims. Believing that advertising can be an instrument for social change, she turns down accounts that conflict with her notion of social responsibility. "We mold opinions," she states, "therefore, we have a responsibility to those people whose opinions we influence." Her company does not advertise alcoholic beverages or cigarettes. She has likewise turned down accounts that she feels are detrimental to the self-esteem of women or blacks. "My belief in the product is unimportant," Proctor muses. "What I resist is the business opportunity to sell questionable or stereotypical products to consumers, especially when there is evidence the product is detrimental or reinforces negative stereotypes."

This incredibly energetic entrepreneur sleeps only two to four hours a day. When asked if she ever gets tired of the hard work and the pushing, she answered, "Of course I do. I feel exploited at times. I feel overworked, misunderstood, misused....All the negatives. My solution is to push those feelings to absurdity. When I realize how absurd it is, and have a great laugh, the feelings are over for another year or so. I never go back and I seldom look back. I've made my share of mistakes and I've learned from them. Energy spent living in the past diminishes your time now and in the future."

Question: Your ethical views in relation to advertising are well known. How do they differ from the business ethics of your competitors?

Proctor: I do not presume to judge anyone's standards but my own. I do believe in the "root-and-fruit" chain of conduct. Whatever you plant or leave behind flowers into something you will see again. You profit or lose by those recurring encounters. So I try to live and utilize my resources in a positive manner.

Question: Are you always pleased with your root-and-fruit chain?

Proctor: When I meet the fruits of my behavior, generally, I am well pleased. Occasionally I have lost revenue because there are some businesses I cannot represent and some people I cannot be comfortable serving. Some businesspeople can separate personal values from business accommodations. I am less complicated and more consistent. There are certain values that remain rock solid with me.

Question: Why has your particular philosophy worked so well for you?

Proctor: Assuming it has—if you mean by that, why do I seem to be more out front than my meager beginning would suggest—I can only express gratitude for that meager beginning. It liberated me in a way that being born in more favored circumstances couldn't have done.

Question: In what way was your meager beginning liberating?

Proctor: I have been poorer, uglier, lonelier, more scared than most people . . . and I survived that childhood. Life has been a piece of cake since I got an education. I have enjoyed the freedom that comes only from knowing what's on the other side. I also know that when we buy inclusion and acceptance with conformity, the price bankrupts us spiritually. My greatest wealth is not financial. It is peace of mind. That shows. And it is infectious.

Question: Is selling different today from what it was 10 or 15 years ago?

Proctor: Selling is not different today. It remains the art and skill of exchanging goods and services for something of negotiated value. What has changed is the marketplace and the attitude of the buyers.

Question: What has changed in the marketplace, in your opinion?

Proctor: With the development of high technology, the buyer is seeing more things, more lifestyles, more options. This places a greater burden on the seller. Not only must a need be generated in order to sell the product but also the buyer must be reinforced in the purchase and conditioned to remain loyal to the choice in the face of newer and more provocative persuasion to make a different decision.

Question: Why do people buy?

Proctor: There are many articulated reasons why people buy: They want something; they need something; a product makes a chore easier; a product makes them more attractive. The basic reason why people buy is the personal gratification they enjoy by successfully negotiating a solution to a perceived problem.

Question: Then why do buyers change their minds when it comes time to repurchase?

Proctor: For the same reason that they bought in the first place. Often they are disappointed with their purchase because the solution requires an internal adjustment. The external purchase alone does not relieve the problem. This does not suggest that the articulated reasons for buying were entirely superficial. Soap is needed to wash clothes clean. The decision making that goes into brand selection, however, reflects the negotiated choice.

Question: In today's economy, are we selling needs or wants?

Proctor: What we are doing, in many cases, is worse than selling needs. We are generating needs. Women are often the victim of this process. Women are perceived as the turnkey of the American economy. We have commercials and programs blaming women for everything from dirty shirt collars to kids' cavities. If everything in a house is there because a woman bought it or contributed to the purchasing decision, then this attack on women is not sexist, per se. One by-product of men's setting up households, which they run alone, and women's waiting until later to marry, is that one-person households are the fastest-growing household segment. Now men too will have their self-esteem tied to plates they can see their face in and shiny floors.

Question: What do you see in the future for working women?

Proctor: Working women are a permanent factor in the American labor force. Not only are they here to stay in the lower "pink ghettos" of labor but also they have been in the line positions for more than five years now and should begin moving into the upper-management levels of industry and the professions.

Question: What do you think awaits them there?

Proctor: If men are objective enough to allow them access, fine, they will be rewarded. If they continue to reject women in top management, more and more women will simply walk away and begin their own businesses.

Women-owned business is the fastest growing segment of all business. Never mind that our little businesses gross, on average, less than $100,000 annually. These women are getting experience, and they are shaking the shackles off their minds. The women starting up and struggling today will soon be joined by their better-trained, better-funded, and more-liberated sisters. This will be an exciting decade.

Question: How have women in the business world changed companies?

Proctor: As far as the big picture goes, women haven't changed much of anything. We are still less than 3 percent of the corporate boards of the industrials and well under 10 percent of top management of top companies overall. And that's where the decision making occurs. On another level, women have made substantive changes in the business ethics, conduct, and philosophy of the companies they work for.

Question: What was the biggest sale you ever made?

Proctor: In 1962 I was an international director for Vee Jay Records in Chicago. While negotiating deals in London, I signed the recording contracts for Vee Jay president E. G. Abner and brought back to America the very first Beatles recording. It amounted to millions of dollars directly and changed American music forever.

Question: What was the most important sale for you personally?

Proctor: After six months of rejection, after rejection from potential clients who had loved me when I was working for someone else but didn't believe a black woman "had it," I landed my first advertising contract with Jewel Foods in Chicago. That was in 1970.

Question: To you, what makes a successful salesperson?
   Proctor: The ability to match your product or service with the needs of the buyer. A successful salesperson must look beyond the resistance. He or she must hear beyond the objections being raised; the successful salesperson must penetrate the wall of withdrawal and touch the buyer where he or she is most in need.

Question: Where do you feel salespeople most often fail?
   Proctor: Too many salespeople attempt to emphasize the quality of the product rather than how it fits into the quality of the buyer's life. They attempt to wear down resistance with insistence. They impress the buyer with knowledge of the product rather than with understanding of the need. Total communication and patience to wait for the perfect time make a successful salesperson.

Question: How do you motivate other people?
   Proctor: I'm not sure I do as good a job of this as I could. Sometimes, I tend to assume that proximity alone is enough. I get frustrated that my people cannot pick up what I'm feeling by osmosis. I feel I can pick up on their vibes. Then I realize that it is a function of the limitation of time. I try to remember that each person in one's life deserves personal time. When I feel that is needed, I give it. People cannot execute a concept they do not understand. Beyond that, sharing the music is the best way to get people to dance.

Question: What motivates you?

Proctor: I have been blessed with the most gentle, supportive human being on earth for a son. I have been fortunate to have touched the lives of many people who have invested in me a lot of their energies, their dreams, their goals. Quite simply, I am needed. There is no greater motivation than that.

ACTION PLAN

- When selling, do more than show customers how your product or services fulfill their needs. Instead, reinforce the buyer's wants and needs throughout the selling process.
- Look beyond customer resistance. Instead of just hearing objections, go deeper by asking probing questions to discover the true needs of the buyer.
- The perfect sale often takes patience. Don't try to wear down the buyer; instead, wait until the buyer shows signs of readiness to close the deal.

CHAPTER 13

GERARD I. NIERENBERG

Why negotiation is really about finding
win-win solutions.

NEGOTIATION IS SO MUCH a part of our daily lives that it is easy to take it for granted. Few of us ever bother to define a negotiation strategy; even fewer are consciously aware of our negotiation philosophy. Most of us employ a hit-and-miss strategy. By trying to get the best deal, we often leave the other person feeling badly or we arrive at agreements that don't last. One thing is sure, not one of us ever wants to feel taken.

Gerard Nierenberg has spent a lifetime studying the subject of negotiation. He has defined negotiation climates, he has analyzed the importance of body language in negotiations, he has developed a unique process for finding a greater number of creative solutions, and much more. His negotiation philosophy is designed to lead to success for all parties. No one need ever feel like the loser in a Nierenberg negotiation because everyone wins.

Nierenberg's guiding philosophy is, simply put, that the purpose of a good negotiation is not how to divide the remaining slice of pie. The purpose is how to make more pie for everyone.

It is a guiding philosophy that creates more for everyone, rather than dividing victor and vanquished. The consequences for business executives are staggering. Without the guiding philosophy of more for everyone, a negotiation will turn into a losing battle.

This is yet another instance in which the person shaped the philosophy and the philosophy shaped a superachiever.

"Your success as a sales professional," suggests Nierenberg, "may well depend on your success as a negotiator." After spending a lifetime as a professional negotiator, he authored the first book on the subject in 1968, *The Art of Negotiating*. He founded the Negotiation Institute, Inc., in New York City, and he began a pioneering effort to define and advance this critical business science. Nierenberg's advice and counsel are sought throughout the world wherever he lectures for business and governments. "Many people think they are sharp negotiators," says Nierenberg, who now has six best-selling books to his credit, "when actually they have only a small number of negotiating techniques at their command."

This interview with Nierenberg shows how his negotiation experience can be applied to selling. As he suggests, "We are involved in negotiating in one form or another each day of our lives." He illustrates his point with this little anecdote: "A few years ago, the president of a large conglomerate came up to me after a seminar on negotiating mergers and acquisitions. He said, 'Jerry, we've been doing pretty well this year, and there is little you can tell me about mergers and acquisitions. We know how to make money. But you told me something important about personal negotiations because I had a discussion with my son before I left this morning, and he told me what I could do with my whole conglomerate.'"

Question: You are a lawyer by training. Did you learn about negotiation in your legal practice?

Nierenberg: This may surprise you, but legal expertise is no help in negotiation. Most lawyers have little training in negotiating other than their own experience. Lawyers are trained as adversaries. In an adversary relationship, you want to win. Practicing law taught me only that many legal victories have little to do with resolving a problem so that it stays resolved. Contracts that end up in court can turn a short-term winner quickly into a long-term loser.

Question: What is the goal of a negotiation relationship compared to an adversary relationship?

Nierenberg: In a negotiation relationship, you want to resolve a problem so that it stays resolved. You want to create an agreement that lasts, where both parties remain satisfied in the long run. In a successful negotiation, everyone wins.

Question: How can everyone win in a competitive society?

Nierenberg: The purpose of competition is to make everyone better, not to kill your competitor. If we would kill all our competitors, we would end up with an unproductive monopoly. Competition brings out the differences, and effective negotiation integrates these differences so that everyone gains. For example, in selling, your competitors teach you how to stay on your toes and remind you that they are going to do more for your customers if you don't do it.

Question: You said once that negotiating is one of the least understood arts in human affairs. What are some of the discoveries you have made that could help us understand more about the negotiation process?

Nierenberg: Well, most people view negotiating as a process where two people are involved in dividing a slice of pie. Their main goal is to get the larger piece. After studying negotiation for more than 17 years, we've come to the conclusion that the goal of a negotiation should not be how to divide the slice of pie but how to make more pie.

Question: When did you create the Negotiation Institute, and how many people have you trained?

Nierenberg: We created the Negotiation Institute in 1966. Its purpose is to expand the knowledge of negotiation and to train negotiators. We do this through our public seminars, in-house seminars, and video and audio tapes. To date, in our public seminars alone, we've trained more than 115,000 people.

Question: You've written several books on the subject. One of your books seems to suggest that we all have a negotiation philosophy whether we are aware of that philosophy or not. Is that correct?

Nierenberg: Yes. One of the strongest forces in our choosing one course of action over another is our philosophy. We need to look at our philosophy occasionally and find out how it is working for us. Our philosophy is made to serve us. We are not made to serve our philosophy.

Question: Let's talk about the profession of selling. What type of philosophy would you recommend for a successful sales negotiation?

Nierenberg: A successful salesperson uses a problem-oriented philosophy. He or she views the prospect's problem as a mutual problem. He or she wants to plan *with* the client, not *for* the client. The other side of the coin would be the salesperson with the game-oriented philosophy. He or she views the prospect as an adversary, someone who must be controlled or manipulated. If you are trying to push or control your prospect, you will only increase his or her defenses and decrease your chances of making the sale.

Question: You are talking about the emotional climate during a sale. How important are feeling in a sales negotiation?

Nierenberg: Let me answer with a question: How do you feel when you realize that the prospect is out to win and make you lose?

Question: I probably would feel antagonized, competitive, or challenged.

Nierenberg: Right. Most people would react that way. You see, in these situations, our emotional defense systems tend to take over. As a consequence, we are tempted to break off communication or want to make the other person lose.

Question: Do you feel we become responsible for the negative climate in this situation?

Nierenberg: I would go further than that; *all* of the climates and feelings that we experience in the negotiating process are of our making.

Question: How can we control the climate in a sales negotiation?

Nierenberg: If I am accusing, judgmental, correcting, or indoctrinating, I will most likely create a defensive prospect. For example, when I tell a prospect that my product is the best in the whole world ..., I am imposing a value judgment that will create a defensive climate.

Question: How can I avoid defensive reactions?

Nierenberg: It's so easy. You can create a supportive climate by being descriptive. You could say, "Our product is currently used by 30,000 customers nationwide." Let the customer appraise your information; don't do it for him or her. Remember, customers want to learn, but they resist being taught.

Question: What if the prospect starts out being defensive?

Nierenberg: It is much easier to change someone who is being defensive to you by being supportive to them, rather than by being defensive to them. You see, when we hit a tennis ball over the net, the kind of spin we put on the ball determines what type of return shot we are going to get. It's the same with negotiation climates. The type of climate you create determines the type of climate you're going to get.

Question: We've talked about how our philosophies influence our negotiations and how the climate contributes to the outcome. How important is nonverbal communication in the negotiation process?

Nierenberg: It is a very important contributing factor. Most salespeople have only a limited awareness of the prospect's body language. The untrained sales negotiator may overlook as much as 50 percent of all nonverbal messages.

Question: How easily can we interpret a prospect's gestures?

Nierenberg: A gesture does not mean anything by itself, unless we put it into a context. In order to understand what's going on, we must observe what I call a "cluster" or group of gestures. We need to watch out for the many shifts and changes before we can see the prospect move from one attitude to another. Also, we need to compare the nonverbal messages to what it said verbally so we can find out if the prospect's body is confirming or denying his or her verbal expressions.

Question: What if the prospect's gestures are inconsistent with the verbal message?

Nierenberg: The nonverbal expressions will give you the prospect's true attitude.

Question: What can we do when we realize that our own bodies communicate a defensive attitude? How can we change it?

Nierenberg: By changing our feelings, we'll automatically change our body language. It's important to read our own gestures during a negotiation. They tell us how we feel, so we can examine the underlying causes. Once we realize what contributed to our defensive attitude, we can go ahead and change it.

Question: How about negotiations on the telephone, where we can't see the prospect's body language?

Nierenberg: Francis Bacon said once, long before the telephone was invented, "If you have something important to communicate, don't write." I say, if you have something important to negotiate, don't call.

Question: Do you feel that people are more impulsive on the telephone than in person?

Nierenberg: No, but we do things on the telephone we never would do in person. It's like when you get behind the wheel of a car and do things to other people that you would never do face to face. Some people are afraid on the telephone, some people become preoccupied with the expense of the call, and others become rash and rude and hang up.

Question: In your book, **The Art of Negotiating,** *you describe many different negotiation techniques like "apparent withdrawal," "feinting," the "salami tactic," or the "crossroads strategy." These techniques sound like guidelines for a game, and yet in your seminars you say that negotiation and life are not games. Aren't you contradicting yourself?*

Nierenberg: Let me clarify this point for you. In a game, you have a limited number of alternatives. In a negotiation, you have an infinite number of alternatives. Games can be played over again, and players can be substituted. Life can't be played over. The rules of a game are given. But what do we know about the rules of life? Think about the many rules prospects make up during a negotiation. Or think about how many prospects actually subscribe to their own rules. Negotiation is not a simple process of sacrificing for the sake of agreement. Negotiation is not an infantile "let's split the difference" proposition. Negotiation is a process of maximizing our interests.

Question: In other words, the experienced negotiator does not view the negotiating process as an "I win—you lose" game.

Nierenberg: Exactly. Amateurs want to play games; professionals want to solve problems so they stay solved.

Question: What is your measure of success?

Nierenberg: To be able to pass on some of my own experiences.

ACTION PLAN

- The purpose of a good negotiation is not to divide the remaining slice of pie. The purpose is to make more pie for everyone.
- The untrained negotiator may overlook as much as 50 percent of all nonverbal messages. Nonverbal expressions hold the key to the prospect's true attitude.
- When we hit a tennis ball over the net, the kind of spin we put on the ball determines the type of return shot we are going to get. It's the same with negotiation climates. The type of climate you create determines the type of climate you're going to get.
- It is easier to change someone's defensive attitude by being supportive than by echoing that person's defensiveness.
- Amateurs want to play games; professionals want to solve problems so they stay solved.

CHAPTER 14

DR. SPENCER JOHNSON

*A doctor turned motivational speaker on how to
measure your success.*

SUCCESSES CAN BE ACHIEVED minute by minute, according to Dr. Spencer Johnson, who is the best-selling co-author of *The One Minute Manager* and *The One Minute Salesperson*. Johnson is well known for his "one-minute" philosophy, but few people realize how many hours, weeks, months, and even years go into his seemingly simple presentation.

If it is true that the easier something appears on the outside, the more work has gone into putting it together, then we can assume that Johnson's one-minute success streak had its roots in years of research and experience. An avid believer in living in the present, Spencer Johnson, a medical doctor by training, practices what he writes, speaks, and preaches. His decision to become a teacher of health rather than a healer of sickness indicates just how far he had to travel away from his initial commitment to medicine.

Johnson now looks upon most illnesses as self-imposed, or at least self-perpetuating. While working in hospitals, Johnson saw hundreds of patients who viewed themselves as victims. They believed nothing could be done for them, and they felt doomed. Those who could accurately assess their own feelings, who took an assertive posture toward their own possibilities for change and growth, no matter what the limitations outside, were the ones who were most likely to become well again. At the very least, they could function successfully within the constraints that were presented.

For those patients who chose to remain victims of circumstances, there was little hope for positive change. Dr. Johnson has explored many different techniques for overcoming self-defeating attitudes. For example, the person who plays the game "I'll be happy when..." is doomed to remain unfulfilled in his or her search for happiness. The person who tells himself or herself that happiness is a state that exists right now is more likely to experience that happiness.

Putting conditions on one's feelings results in poor performance and poor feelings. Setting up conditional happiness, success, or other outcomes leads to ever-increasing feelings of frustration. But setting up dual happiness, happiness for both now and later, allows for good moments at any time.

Johnson's technique of living in the present doesn't allow negative attitudes to fester. A setback is only one moment in time. It ends. The next moment is up to you, says Johnson. Make that next moment one of learning and the growth will happen by and of itself. Before you know it, you will be where you wanted to be from the start.

Spencer Johnson has been an inspiration to millions of us to live now, to be happy with who we are now, and to allow ourselves to grow in the future. There is no justification, in Johnson's view, for hanging on to old wounds and miseries. Johnson himself has had his share of hard knocks. He even mentioned, in passing, the pain of failed relationships. But he would not allow himself to dwell on those past failures—to live as if they were still alive.

His lesson is subtle. His words seem glib. Hidden within the message is a pioneering effort to lift the collective spirit and to let it fly free.

Question: How do you explain the phenomenal success of your book **The One Minute Manager?**

Johnson: Most people are overwhelmed by the amount of information in this overcommunicative society. *The One Minute Manager* became so successful because it tells people something very simple—something that works!

Question: What is that?

Johnson: Well, it tells them how to manage in a simple way that they can use immediately. Also, the timing was good because businesspeople were looking for good management techniques.

Question: How did you make the complex transition from physician to author and motivator?

Johnson: Working with patients in a hospital, I always saw bad attitudes. I became convinced that bad attitudes can create illness. I realized that if you could make yourself ill, you could make yourself well. And I thought, "Why am I going to spend 50 years helping people after they've gotten sick? Why not help them to see that they can do things with their minds to keep themselves well?"

Question: What did you perceive was making them sick?

Johnson: These hospital patients had one thing in common. They all viewed themselves as victims—as under the control of something outside of themselves.

Question: In a world that often victimizes people, how can you not view yourself as a victim?

Johnson: As long as you view yourself that way, you can't. If you think the world victimizes you, you're in trouble. The reality is that nobody cares one way or the other about you. So they are not really victimizing you. But if you view it that way, then that gives them power over you. If you can learn to view the world in positive, upbeat terms, then even when bad things seem to be happening to you, you can realize that it's only for a limited time. The question then is do you go down or not?

Question: Would you agree with Zig Ziglar's statement that you'd better be tough with yourself or the world will be tough on you?

Johnson: I would agree with that if he would insert the word "behavior." It's good to be tough on your behavior but it's very unwise to be tough on yourself. In *The One Minute Salesperson*, Larry Wilson and I talk about praising yourself within the context of a self-management system. Praising yourself for doing something right can be a strong antidote to self-talk that is overly tough.

Question: Does anyone have the power to tell you whether you're O.K. or not?

Johnson: No one has the power to say whether I'm O.K. or not. I alone have that power. The point is—we're all O.K.

Question: So that's a given....

Johnson: Absolutely—that's not up for grabs. Even if you fall below your sales quota, that's not who you are. You are not your sales. You are the person behind your sales....

Question: How does your book **The Precious Present** *relate to salespeople?*

Johnson: I suspect that I'm like a lot of salespeople in that they don't need to get any better than they are right now. They don't need to learn anything. They can have a gift simply by enjoying the present. Salespeople who work in the present do better work. They don't divide their energy with worry over the next sale, or yesterday's missed opportunity. When all your energy is focused on the here and now, you're more productive.

Question: What did you anticipate the reception of this book would be?

Johnson: It never occurred to me that business executives and sales managers would buy *The Precious Present*. I saw it as a general book. But now I see that business executives need to be reminded not to carry each successive problem around all day long. You can solve a problem and move on and forget the past one.

Question: Have you achieved all your goals?

Johnson: I hope not.

Question: Are goals important?

Johnson: Well, I fell into the trap of "I'm going to be happy when..." I set all kinds of goals and then expected that upon reaching one, the next one would make me happy. I remember playing tennis and looking up at the hill beyond the club and thinking, "I'd love to have a house on the hill." I played lousy tennis and I delayed getting the house on the hill.

Question: Did you ever get your house on the hill?

Johnson: Yes, I did, but not until I started to appreciate what I had and didn't compare it to what I thought I wanted. It wasn't until I started to live in "the precious present" that I became the most productive and profitable.

Question: How did you sell your first book to a publisher?

Johnson: [*Chuckles.*] That's where I learned my first lesson in sales and marketing. I had a manuscript called *Fraternity Row*, and I sent it around to all kinds of publishers in New York, and I just couldn't make a sale. So I decided to package it, which was a new idea to me. And finally I realized that everyone loves a winner, so I packaged it as if it was already a winner. I went to a well-known actor named Dick Powell, and I asked him to write a foreword for my book.

Question: How did you know him?

Johnson: I didn't—I just knocked on his door at the studio where he worked.

Question: And he let you in?

Johnson: No, he told me to go away.

Question: What did you do then?

Johnson: I told him, "Look, I don't want to get into motion pictures. I don't want a job." So he said, "In that case come on in."

Question: That's a terrific cold-call technique.

Johnson: I told him I was a fraternity brother, and sure enough he read the book, liked it, and wrote the foreword. Then I sent his foreword to 13 other very famous people and asked them if they would comment on what they thought of college fraternities. And they did.

Question: How can salespeople approach the problem of the overloaded prospect who just doesn't want to look at one more product?

Johnson: Well, first that salesperson has to be sold on himself or herself. Then you must think of the other person. What are you bringing to him or her that will interest him or her. People don't care about what's important to you. They care about what's important to them.

Question: What do you have to know to be good in sales?

Johnson: There are certain techniques that the outstanding salesperson seems to use automatically, like visualization and projection. And of course timing and a good sense of when to close and when to stand back. One of the best ways to realize how good you are is to catch yourself doing something right.

Question: What is your measure of success?

Johnson: My measure of success is how peaceful you are with yourself regardless of what's going on around you. But my measure used to revolve around goals. I would set a goal and go after it. If I got the goal, I felt I was a success. If I didn't get the goal, I felt frustrated. The problem with making your happiness dependent on a goal is that when you achieve that goal, you're bound to say, "Is that all there is?"

Question: What about happiness?

Johnson: Happiness is right now. If you're not happy right now, you're never going to be happy. If you can't be happy right now, even if things don't look too good, you're never going to be able to make things just the way you want them. That's the great message in *The Precious Present*.

Question: What is the advantage of living in the present?

Johnson: Once you start savoring and accepting what you are and what is happening in the present, you get enormous personal power and energy. This is particularly true in sales. Salespeople who are not together themselves make customers anxious and defensive. They won't let those salespeople in, and they won't buy from them either.

Question: Do you see a division between past, present, and future?

Johnson: No, there is none. There is only the present. Life is a series of present moments.

Question: What is the present like for a salesperson who has just lost a sale?

Johnson: He's probably down. He's *not* living in the present. He's very into what he thinks it ought to be. He can't change anything about that sale. He can't go back and grab the prospect by the throat. But he can say to himself, "Right now is a very good moment in my life. And there's a purpose but I just don't know what it is yet. I will learn something from this." If you see each selling experience as part of a continuum, it will energize you. If you don't see it that way, you get demoralized. And you go into your next sales call down.

Question: Why don't we live in the present?

Johnson: Most of us were not trained to live in the present. We were trained to get ready.

Question: Do you ever procrastinate?

Johnson: I'm doing it right now. I don't always live in the present. I don't always do what I know. I don't think any of us do. But the more often I do it, the better my life works. Procrastination is the worry about the future.

Question: How can salespeople reconcile their need for the immediate gratification of a sale and the management part of selling, like follow-up and paperwork?

Johnson: Everybody has a problem with that. I constantly get asked, "What about planning for the future?" My answer to that is to be in that moment. Even if that moment is paperwork or planning. Then you won't be living in the future. Realize that paperwork is part of selling. If you view a sale as only that fraction of a second when the customer says yes, then you're going to view everything else as a waste of time.

Question: In other words, there's more to love than just sex.

Johnson: Exactly. You'll miss some very enjoyable moments if you view it that way. And if you do paperwork out of resentment and boredom, guess how much you're going to learn from it. But if you reflect on what you did on each sales call as you do the paperwork connected to it—if you use your paperwork as a time to reflect on your behavior—then paperwork will become a fabulous tool, a self-learning tool.

Question: What does it take to do that?

Johnson: It takes a great attitude. And winners are people with great attitudes.

Question: Can salespeople choose their own role models?

Johnson: Oh, of course. Most of us don't realize how many choices we have all the time. The key is awareness—being aware of the choice you are making right now. Salespeople have some of the greatest number of choices to make since most of the time, nobody knows where they are. Their managers have a general idea where they ought to be, but salespeople are out there making choices all day long.

Question: Have you had role models?

Johnson: I've had a lot of role models over the years. I like to learn from what works so I watch it and try to do the same thing. That comes back to seeing the movie in your mind—visualization. You see it before it happens. One of my best role models is Ken Blanchard. He's the expert on the psychology of plenty.

Question: Recent hospital studies have shown that people who are cynical actually have shorter life spans.

Johnson: That goes back to my early experience in medicine. The cynics spent all their time in and out of hospitals. And you can even hear that if you listen to them for a little bit of time. The cynicism actually breaks down the body. It's just fascinating how we program ourselves for what happens in our lives.

ACTION PLAN

- Look for ways to make something complicated simple.
- Learn to see the world in a positive way.
- Practice positive self-talk. Praise yourself when you do something right.
- Know when to close and when to stand back.
- Look at each sales call as part of a continuum. Let this energize you.

Index

~∾———————∾~

About the Author

©Hisham Bharoocha

A DUAL CITIZEN of both Austria and the United States, Gerhard Gschwandtner is the founder and publisher of *Selling Power*, the leading magazine for sales professionals worldwide, with a circulation of 165,000 subscribers in 67 countries.

He began his career in his native Austria in the sales training and marketing departments of a large construction equipment company. In 1972, he moved to the United States to become the company's North American Sales Training Director, later moving into the position of Marketing Manager.

In 1977, he became an independent sales training consultant, and in 1979 he created an audiovisual sales training course called "The Languages of Selling." Marketed to sales managers at Fortune 500 companies, the course taught nonverbal communication in sales together with professional selling skills.

In 1981, Gerhard launched *Personal Selling Power*, a tabloid-format newsletter directed to sales managers. Over the years the tabloid grew in subscriptions, size, and frequency. The name changed to *Selling Power*, and in magazine format it became the leader in the professional sales field. Every year *Selling Power* publishes the "Selling Power 500," a listing of the 500 largest sales forces in America. The company publishes books, sales training posters, and audio and video products for the professional sales market.

Gerhard has become America's leading expert on selling and sales management. He conducts webinars for such companies as SAP, and *Selling Power* has recently launched a new conference division that sponsors and conducts by-invitation-only leadership conferences directed toward companies with high sales volume and large sales forces.

For more information on *Selling Power* and its products and services, please visit www.sellingpower.com.

Subscribe to *Selling Power* today and close more sales tomorrow!

GET 10 ISSUES – INCLUDING THE SALES MANAGER'S SOURCE BOOK.

In every issue of *Selling Power* magazine you'll find:

■ **A Sales Manager's Training Guide** with a one-hour sales training workshop complete with exercises and step-by-step instructions. Get a new guide in every issue! Created by proven industry experts who get $10,000 or more for a keynote speech or a training session.

■ **Best-practices reports** that show you how to win in today's tough market. Valuable tips and techniques for opening more doors and closing more sales.

■ **How-to stories** that help you speed up your sales cycle with innovative technology solutions, so you'll stay on the leading edge and avoid the "bleeding edge."

■ **Tested motivation ideas** so you and your team can remain focused, stay enthusiastic and prevail in the face of adversity.

Plus, you can sign up for five online SellingPower.com newsletters absolutely FREE.

for any Sales Career

201 Super Sales Tips

The Pocket Sales Mentor

The Pocket Guide to Selling Greatness

The Ultimate Sales Training Workshop

Secrets of Superstar Sales Pros

The Art of Nonverbal Selling

McGraw-Hill books are available at special quantity discounts to use as premiums and sales promotions, or for use in corporate training programs. For more information please contact us at bulksales@mcgraw-hill.com, or contact your local bookstore.